Buckshot's C
Trapping Guide

A compilation of 34 years of trapping experience.

Written by Bruce 'Buckshot' Hemming

Copyright © 2009 Bruce 'Buckshot' Hemming

All rights reserved worldwide. No part of this book may be reproduced in any form or by any electronic or mechanical means, including information storage and retrieval systems, without written permission from the author and publisher, except by a reviewer who may quote brief passages in review.

Published by: Bruce 'Buckshot' Hemming
6441 61st Street
Gackle, N.D. 58442

Editorial Director: Max Burnett

Cover Design: Max Burnett

Book Design: Bruce 'Buckshot' Hemming
and Max Burnett

157 pages; soft cover

ISBN# 978-0-578-01885-0

Printed in the

United States of America

Warning

The information contained in this book reflects the author's personal experiences with particular tools, mechanisms, materials and procedures.

These experiences occurred under specific circumstances that the reader and other persons cannot duplicate exactly.

Therefore, the author, publisher and distributor of this book disclaim any liability for any damage or injury of any kind that may result from the use of misuse of the information contained in this book.

It is the reader's and other persons' responsibility to wear proper protective equipment, exercise caution and to read, understand and follow all applicable safety and related rules, guidelines, regulations and laws when using any tools, mechanisms, or operating any machinery.

This book is for informational purposes only.

Table of Contents

Dedication

I would like to thank Max Burnett for his time and dedication in helping me to edit and smooth out this book. Without his help, it would never have made it into print.

Preface

My first trapping book "Buckshot's Modern Trapping Guide", is widely known throughout the world as the première trapping book to have for survival. I wrote that book ten years ago, and today, in the used book market, it is selling for as high as 15 times the original price. When I discovered that, and considered the constant stream of emails from people across the country, I decided it was time to put an updated version on the market.

I have learned a great deal more since writing that first book, and now gladly share all that I know with you. I'll show you the inside tricks of the trade that have taken me a lifetime to learn. The value of this book represents the culmination of my 34 years of trapping experience to date. How do you put a price tag on that? At a guess, it would cost over $30,000.00 to pay for the training, the books, the equipment and the truck repairs I have experienced on my journey (grin). Lucky for you, you don't have to invest 34 years or $30,000.00 to learn trapping and snaring from the school of hard knocks. Instead, you can simply buy this book and skip all the myths and misinformation, and step right into the shoes of the modern trapper.

I believe America is currently heading toward a Great Depression, and that there is a real need for a small percentage of folks to step forward and walk out "into the wilds" to survive. God be with you all on this journey.

My favorite quote is from the famous Mountain Man, Kit Carson. Quoted over a century ago, he said: "The best years of my life were spent trapping." May the spirit of the wild touch your soul as you walk the path and follow the traditions of the true Mountain Man.

Bruce 'Buckshot' Hemming

Chapter 1: Welcome to Trapping - You are going to Love it

You wake up just before sunrise, excited about the prospects of the day ahead of you. You dress quickly, gaze at your sleeping partner and step outside. The cool air hits your face and the frost crunches under your feet. You look out at the brilliant colors; the brilliant orange and yellow, and your senses are on full alert as you approach your first trap. The excitement builds as you spot a fox running in a circle at your set. A secret smile spreads across your face. You have caught a beautiful, prime red fox. You have just outsmarted one of the most difficult animals to trap and you know, beyond a shadow of a doubt, that you are on your way to becoming a successful trapper. You look past the first set and see yet another fox running a circle at your second set…you just caught your first double, and on red fox too! You quickly dispatch the animals and remake the sets. There are experienced trappers who have spent years waiting for the awesome feeling of a double on red fox, and here it is right before your very eyes.

You load them in the truck and prepare to walk down to the farm pond where you have muskrat and raccoon sets. You realize that it doesn't matter if you catch anything else today. You just caught your first double on red fox and the world is looking good. You know you will remember every detail of this day - the look of the sky, the bite in the air, the smell of the earth, and the exact location of your sets. You snap a picture of the red foxes so you can relive this exciting day whenever you want to.

As you quietly but confidently approach the pond, your steps are light and the smile won't seem to go away. The surface of the pond is a steely gray; a raccoon is laying half out of the bucket you prepared - the #220 Conibear did its job. Feeling that this is one of those days where everything is going your way, you walk out to check your muskrat traps. The bank dens are covered with #110 Conibears and as you approach, you see a rat-tail floating near the surface of the pond…another catch. You remake the set and toss the muskrat in your pack. The next three sets are empty, but then a surprise catch at the next one really makes your day.

Instead of a smooth rat-tail floating near that one you see a fluffy tail. You almost trip and fall in the water as you try a little too hard to reach the trap to retrieve your very first mink. You carefully pull the mink up and find you are smiling from ear to ear. You think to yourself, "Mr. Mink, your muskrat killing days are over". The glossy black fur gleams as it reflects the first rays of sunlight. You remake the set, hoping that maybe, just maybe, you'll get lucky and catch another mink here. You pick up two more muskrats as you complete your small starting trap-line. What a day! Two fox, one raccoon, a mink and three muskrats. You feel especially proud because you know you're just starting out and you realize all over again how happy you are to have decided to learn the art of trapping.

Like both hunting and fishing, in trapping some days everything goes right - other days everything goes wrong. And while you learn to take the good with the bad, you live for those days when everything goes right. It's an exciting time of year to be out in the woods. You study nature books from the library and conduct late-night web searches to learn everything you can about the animals you want to trap. You're smart enough to know that you must learn to understand each animal you want to trap, and that understanding comes only from study and experience. All spring and summer you spend some of your free time learning about muskrats, mink, raccoons, red fox, coyotes, beaver and otter. You strike up relationships with local farmers so you can gain permission to trap on their land.

In the summer, you'll go out and spend many an evening watching the pond near your home to see the muskrat swimming around. Where are they going? Why do they climb up on one log in the water and not the other? You begin to look for details that you never took time for in the past. The animals themselves will be your best teachers; showing you how they travel, what makes them stop and why they choose to sit on a certain log.

You can spend years observing animals and after a while you'll begin to notice that certain patterns emerge. The most important lesson you need to learn is 'why' they do what they do. Why are foxes traveling here and not there? Why do I see raccoon tracks near the pond but also out in the cornfield? Where are the apple trees on the property? How about wild grapes, wild cherries, and berry patches? You will learn the natural food sources for each animal. If the food is there, the animals will most likely be there as well. You have to learn to 'be' the animal you want to trap. After chasing animals in the woods for 34 years, I still learn something new every year. I like to think of this as refining the little details.

"The Trapper" comes from a proud tradition of the early American Mountain Man. They were truly free men that walked off into the wilderness to challenge themselves in the truest test of courage, manhood and skills. If you got sick or injured, no one was coming to your aid. Your very survival depended on the skills you brought with you and those you were savvy enough to pick up along the way. Trapping beaver and other critters was worth cash money but for every man that actually became rich trapping beaver, there were countless others pursuing a pipe dream. In his later years, Kit Carson said the happiest days of his life were the ones he spent trapping. You will see wonders of nature that even today few other people will ever see.

Although there are as many different kinds of trapping as there are trappers, my favorite kind is canoe trapping on a small river. Shortly after you push off in that canoe, you leave behind not only the stress but also the sound of modern civilization. Just as it was 200 years ago, it' just you against the elements…raw, pure, nothing artificial added! It'll be just you, the wilderness and the adventure ahead. And yes, it's one big adventure. Sure, you'll have wet feet, cold hands and frustrations galore. But you'll also experience success and those hard cold obstacles will seem light years away as you proudly walk in the footsteps of the Mountain Men that came before you. Trappers are a rare breed - hardy, good natured, hard workers. And did I mention hard work? But, to me there is no better work than to provide for yourself and your family while enjoying the wonders of Mother Nature. How can it get any better than that?

I have witnessed nature's raw power in the middle of a fierce snowstorm, and a few times I came close to not making it home. But, as I look back over more than three decades of trapping, I would not trade my worst day in the woods or on the water for my best day in the city. There is nothing I cherish more than the ongoing opportunity to walk the road of the modern Mountain man lifestyle. So now, I invite you to come along and learn the art of trapping. Catch the spirit of the wild. Throw off the shackles of civilization. Shoulder your pack, grab your .22 rifle and start this adventure with me. I promise you your life will never be the same once you become…a trapper.

Here is a list of all the animals I have trapped in my lifetime.

short tail weasel	long tail weasel	mink
Muskrats	opossums	armadillos
ground hog	snapping turtles	beaver
otter	fisher	bobcats
blue fox	accidental ducks	squirrels
badgers	raccoons	skunks
accidental frog	ground squirrels	gophers
porcupines	gray fox	red fox
coyotes	rabbits	mongoose
feral pigs	fish	mice
brown rats	accidental black bear cub	

Chapter 2: Trapping Equipment

The first thing you need to do is forget everything you think you know about trapping and animals and re-start your thinking the right way. Understanding positive and negative electric current does not make you an electrician that can re-wire a house. What you think you know about trapping can lead you down many a false path and waste your time. Trappers can be a funny lot. As a rule, they don't like to share their little tips and tricks about trapping. Then there's the intentionally wrong information put out there with the sole purpose of leading you down the wrong path. As an example, think about all the importance placed on keeping everything 100% scent-free. While it's true you need to be careful with scent, in reality, if you worried more about wind direction than human scent you'd be a far better trapper. Some things you might hear seem to make a lot of common sense, but you can't always rely on common sense with trapping. Most of the time, it's better to rely on your 'learned' sense.

The best source for information is to contact your local Department of Natural Resources or fish and game department. Ask for the list of animals that can be trapped in your area and for any publications they have on animal studies. You would be surprised by the amount of information you can get for free. But, let's break things down into three categories. Michigan is a real good state, for example. In Southern Michigan, you have mostly farmland. Here, you'll find farmland animals like skunks, opossums, raccoons, ground hogs, muskrat, mink, fox and coyotes. But, you're not likely to see many beaver or otter, and definitely no fishers or bobcats.

Now the Upper Peninsula of Michigan is mostly wild lands where you will find fisher, beaver, otter, and bobcats. You see, the land has changed and the animals have changed along with it. Let's break it down to farmland trapping, deep woods trapping and urban trapping. Now if I were to ask you where to find the most animals per square mile what would you say? If you thought the deep woods, you'd be completely wrong. See why I said forget everything you think you know? Animals are just like humans. They need all the same basic survival conditions; food, water, shelter, and mates. A wilderness area in Upper Michigan might have three raccoons per square mile, while a Southern Michigan farmland area might have 24 coons per square mile and a suburb might have 50 coons per square mile! The main reason for this is weather conditions and food sources. The deep long cold winter of the Upper Peninsula thins out the coons. But the southern farmland has good woods cover for shelter, great food sources in the corn fields, and easier winters, so naturally just based on this knowledge you can see why the raccoon population is higher in the farmland areas. But why such high numbers in the city?

For the exact same reason: plenty of food from outside dog and cat dishes, garbage dumps and uncovered outside residential trash containers. Think of all the places for coons to shelter in a city with a million people living in it. In culverts, abandoned buildings, warehouses etc… There is a big trapping lesson here, so pay attention. The more food sources there are in a given area, the more critters there will be. I hope the light bulb just clicked on in your mind.

Now you need to decide what kind of trapper you want to be. Once you have made up your mind, you will need to know what kind of equipment you need to buy. For instance, are you trapping in an urban area for profit? If so, a great source of income can come from trapping problem animals like ground hogs, coons and squirrels. Now this is where understanding equipment is vital.

Think of all the different traps, snares, and live cage traps as different tools. Kind of like a machinist hammer, a carpenter hammer and a roofing hammer. Each hammer will work for driving a nail, but each has its intended purpose and is best used for what it was designed to do. Think of traps, snares and cage traps in much the same way. Each is a special tool designed for a specific use.

Now, let's say you want to get started trapping pest animals for profit. You will need an assortment of cage traps from the small squirrel size to the large coon size. But, you will also need some snares and traps for certain spots. The main problems with pest control trapping are people and their animals. Dogs and cats are a pain and will ruin your sets, eat your bait and generally cause hardship and aggravation for you, the trapper. To avoid this you have to have a real good understanding of animal habits to avoid catching these problem critters. That's why I do NOT recommend that beginners get into pest control trapping around the cities, until they have enough experience and understand the art of trapping different types of animals.

I will say this more than once because it's very important; you are only as good a trapper as your equipment will let you be. Buy the best equipment, maintain it properly and you will have a much greater chance of becoming a successful trapper. Forget all the mickey-mouse nonsense about homemade single strand snares and deadfalls. If you want to start catching critters right away, then listen up. Good equipment and technique equals success. If you want to play with sticks, rocks and strings then, you've just bought the wrong book. This book teaches methods to help make you a successful trapper.

Now let's take a look at all the different types of traps. You will start with the leg restraining type. The new modern ones have smooth jaws and the most popular are coil spring traps that come in the following sizes: #1, #1-1/2, #1-3/4, #2, #3, #4 and #5. With long spring traps, there are sizes #0, #1, #1-1/2, #2, #3, #4, #5 and of course all the way up to bear sized traps. The picture  above right shows a #1 longspring. Notice that the chain is attached opposite of the spring. That causes the animal to pull toward the spring, which increases your catch count. Conibears, or body gripping traps, come in sizes #110, #120, #160, #220, #280, #330 and #660.

This picture compares a #1 longspring to a #4 longspring.

Here you can see the #1 set. Note that the pan is level with the lever post

#1-3/4 Northwoods Coil spring. Note the trap is laminated with #9 wire for better holding power. Square jaw traps are the best.

Note with the #9 wire the jaw thickness almost doubles increasing the holding power on the animals leg.

There are literally hundreds of different kinds of snares, but lets just stick with the basics for now. There are three different types of snare locks. First, there's the relaxing lock, which is designed to snare the animal without killing it. Then there's the kill lock, which is designed to kill the animal. Finally, the spring assisted kill lock, which kills the animal quickly and humanely.

Conibears are by far are the easiest to understand and will quickly get you catching animals right away, but they have their disadvantages. They are strictly a kill trap. If you happen to accidentally catch someone's dog or cat, then they're not only caught, but also very dead. However, you can avoid this problem by setting your trap in the right location. I'll cover this a little further on in the book. Modified leg restraining traps are better in certain spots because you can release <u>most</u> animals caught in them unharmed.

So, let's start out with a basic kit for catching the animals like at the beginning of this article. If you're in an area with just red fox and no Coyotes, all you need is about six #1-1/2 coil spring traps. That is a great general-purpose trap that will catch red fox, ground hogs, opossums, skunks, coons, mink and muskrats. I'll discuss trap modifications for these later on. Now, a coyote is too big and strong for that trap, so if you want to cover all your bases, the #1-3/4 is the trap of choice for the open farmland set. Use the #1-1/2 for water sets for mink, coon and muskrats. Use

#160 or #220 conibears for taking raccoons, badgers and ground hogs.

#110 conibears are the best survival traps on the market, bar none. One dozen in your pack will keep you in meat. If you want a small game trap, then the #110 conibear is the trap for you. It'll take rabbits, squirrels, mink, muskrat, fish, birds, and even frogs. Now, if you have some beaver around, a couple of #330 conibears should do the trick. *The picture on the right shows a #330 ready to go. I removed the chain and installed a swivel to hook the wire onto.* Nothing will get you on a farmer's good side any better than trapping out those pesky beaver that are flooding his corn fields. If snaring is legal in your area, you could use some relaxing lock snares on the farm to set up for coon and fox.

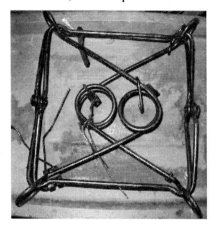

Snares

A whole book could be dedicated just to snares and all the different types. The modern snare is made from aircraft cable in 7x7 or 1x19 galvanized cable. Sizes range from the tiny 3/64", 1/16", 5/64", 3/32" and 1/8". I'll keep things simple and easy for you to understand. The tiny 3/64" cable is more of a specialty cable for small critters like mink and muskrats. It has the advantage of closing quicker and if you just want to specialize in mink, it would be a good choice. But I look at things differently. I want a cable size that will successfully catch a variety of animals. The 1/16" small game snare will catch rabbits, squirrels, mink, muskrats, marmots and ground hogs. The same for the 5/64". If you just want a fast fox snare this may be a good choice, but if you want the most from your snares the 3/32" will catch coons, beaver, fox, coyotes, and with the right lock even feral pigs. It can also be used as an 'emergency only' deer snare and even to take small black bears up to 200 pounds. Now if you have large hogs over 200 pounds up to about 300 pounds, the better choice would be 1/8 inch cable. But overall, 1/16" and 3/32" will handle most of your snaring needs.

7x7 is by far the best for general use. The 1x19 has one main advantage: it will form a better round loop. But the big disadvantage is it won't store very well and can be deformed easily during storage. Anything tossed carelessly on it will kink the cable or deform it. It's a very touchy cable to work with. One advantage is with under the ice beaver snaring you can use the 1x19 in 1/16" cable because the beaver is dead really quick. But, if you try to trap a beaver in open water they will break it and escape.

I like to keep things simple so I stick with 7x7 with aluminum ends because the aluminum end smashes into the galvanized cable better. In fact, the cable will break before the aluminum stops will give. But, steel stops can slip off the cable if not put on correctly. Stainless steel cable is bad news. It won't dull up, and animals will shy away from it.

There are many choices to make on equipment, but hear me loud and clear on this point; Victor's are not the best traps on the market. Yes, I said that Victor is just a brand name and not the best trap on the market. They are under new ownership now but in the 70's, 80's and early 90's, Victor coil spring traps were some of the worst junk on the market. They had weak steel and poor design along with cheap springs. If you choose to use them, they will cost you a ton in lost fur. Notice that I said coil springs. The long spring Victors are good traps. Sleepy Creek traps

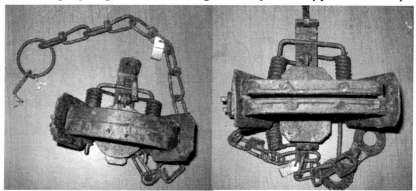

(pictured above left) are made in America and are good traps. Note the drowning lock attacked to the chain. Cut that off and install a universal swivel. It will work as a drowner lock or use a ½" rebar stake. Plus you have the swivel for more animal comfort. To the right of the sleepy creek is a modified #3

Bridger. Note the square jaw and high levers, with double stake swivel added.

Dukes are good, but Bridger coil springs are my favorites. BMI is also a good choice. I think with Conibears, the better choices are Bridger, Sleepy creek, BMI and Dukes, in that order. They will all catch you animals. My favorite traps are made by the old Northwoods trap company, but they are no longer available. The Northwoods #1 - ½ , #1 ¾, #2 and #3 coil spring square jaws are some of the best traps ever made. Today, Bridger is the only one that is real close in the square jaw design.

Well, since I slammed Victor I'll also praise them. Their long spring traps are some of the best on the market. If you find some old Blake and Lamp traps in good shape, buy them if you can afford them because they're a great trap. Newhouse's are awesome traps but most people nowadays know they are collector items and they are hard to get.

Thompson snares are a good brand and I have nothing bad to say about them, but in *my* opinion, they aren't worth the extra money for a name. One warning on snares - anyone with $10 can open a web site and start selling snares. Make sure you know you're buying from someone that actually knows how to make snares. In the last 10 years, I can't even begin to name all the snare companies that have come and gone on the web. Most have no business experience and jump right in and sell snares for 6 months until the complaints are flowing in, then they close down shop. You get what you pay for. Is that $2 - $3 you save on a dozen really worth it? Let's face it, when you find parts missing and cheap, poor quality cable with a slow reacting snare that lose more than they catch, how can you justify that just for the sake of saving money? Because if you really think about it, that $2 - $3 you saved on the snares can cost you hundreds in lost fur and if your survival depends on your snares, it could cost you your life.

How much equipment do I need?

It's very important for you to understand the principles and techniques leading to successful trapping and snaring. And once you have a little experience under your belt, there's no reason why you shouldn't do very well as a trapper. Starting out, I would expect you to average at least one catch for every four sets checked. That's just a ballpark figure, because there are a lot of variables to consider when trapping. While running a fox trapline, you may average one catch for every ten sets. With coyotes, you may average one catch for every fifty sets. On muskrat, however, you might have one catch for every two traps. Your success will be determined by many factors concerning location, bait, type of sets used, weather and time of year etc…

The secret to successful trapping is changing locations and setting one new trap each day. Sounds funny doesn't it? Just one trap a day. Let me tell you a story. I was trapping this small wood lot using the useless victor #1 - 1/2 coilspring trap. A monster coon powered out of the trap right away. It happens a lot with the victor coilspring; that's why I don't like them. I made a new set 50 yards away and two days later there sat the big coon; a 25 pounder. How did I know it was the same coon? I knew because I could see the hair on the paw missing where he pulled out of the first trap. One new trap saved the day. If you were paying attention, I just gave you some really valuable information. Did you catch it? Coons don't become trap shy as much as location shy. I have seen this many times while raccoon trapping. Simply moving a trap or making a new set will get you back in fur.

One study found that coons travel in a group averaging 3 - 4 coons. So if you set one trap or snare, you catch one coon. The others see the caught coon and most of the time will avoid that location for a while. Sometimes for as long as a year. But if you set 3 - 6 traps or snares, you might get lucky and catch all 3 or 4 coons at the same time. That means that you don't have to worry about educating other coons in the same group. I've found that with coons (depending on where you live), just moving your trap a few feet away from the previous trap circle can get you back in coon fur. That may not always work, but it's worth a try.

So you've gone to the trouble to buy my book. What is your goal as a trapper? What kind of trapper do you hope to become? Will it be just for fun, as a hobby? Or maybe to make a little extra money? Most importantly, are you trying to discover new ways to insure your survivability if this great country of ours becomes unstable? Lots of questions, I know. But if you answered yes to any of the above questions, then you made a wise decision when you bought this book. I will teach you what you need to know, but I'll go a step further as well. I'll share the secrets that have helped make me successful. If you are to practice your survival skills and secure a few pelts to tan each year, then start with four #110 conibears and 1 dozen small game snares and go out and play each year and learn. Now what will you need to stock up on for the end of the world scenario? A minimum to start with is 10 - dozen small game snares, 6 - dozen medium game snares and 4 - dozen camlock snares. Add 1- dozen #110, four #220 and two #330 conibears, along with a setting tool for the conibears and six #1 - 3/4 modified 4-coil traps.

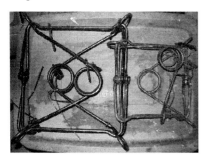

To the left is a picture showing the size difference between the #330 and #220.The picture on the right shows the size difference between the #330 and #110. The #110 is small, light and easy to carry, having only one spring.

Now if you want to specialize and make some money, and you already have a good muskrat trapping place, you could get 300 traps - 150 #110 conibears and 150 #1 longsprings. Actually, a part-timer could start with 3 - dozen #110 conibears and 1 - dozen #1 long springs. That will be plenty of traps for you to run, and experience will teach you that for yourself. 1 - dozen #1 - 3/4 square jaw modified 4 coiled traps and 1 - dozen snares will cover just about anywhere in the US for a good well rounded trapline.

Now with predator trapping, a pro is going to be running 100 - 150 traps or more at a time. The plan is to take at least ten animals a day along a 100-mile trapline.But even with an area that large, you are going to be changing to a new location every week to ten days.

What are some good ways to buy traps on the cheap? Well, a really good way to get your first traps is to run a want-ad in the local newspaper asking for used traps. You will be surprised how much equipment you can come up with using this method. A friend of mine did this and an old timer sold him a really nice collection of fifty traps that included three Newhouses. He bought the entire batch for $150, and turned around and re-sold two of the Newhouses for $400! He kept one of the Newhouses as a collectors item. So not only did this add 48 traps to his collection, but he made a $250 profit to boot. Not everyone is going to get that lucky, but you can find some really good deals if you get out there and beat the brush. I hit a garage sale once and bought a pack basket, 1 - dozen muskrat stretchers, three mink stretchers, 2 - dozen #1 longsprings and 6 underspring #1 for $45. I have other friends that bought all kinds of equipment used with great results as well; fleshing knives, fleshing beams, stretchers and traps...the works. So get out there and find that one person with a garage full of old traps, and you too can hit the lottery.

Now if you're going to trap some critters on individually owned property in the city, you will need a good collection of live traps. You can make some real good money if you can track down the people that own the property. I don't recommend that you try nuisance trapping until you have 2 - 3 years experience. Otherwise, you can embarrass yourself and drive yourself out of the market for a good while. And always be sure to comply with the trapping laws in your state. Dealing with people who want the animals removed without harming them can be a little tricky at times. In most states, you have to put the animal down, because if you release them, they have a habit of showing up and becoming a nuisance to someone else's property and the trouble starts all over again. Plus, you will have a trap shy animal that is going to be a lot harder to trap the next time.

When dry land trapping, a 5-gallon bucket with a work pouch on it is awesome for hauling your supplies in. The tools you'll need at a minimum is: a trowel, a dirt sifter, large hammer, and if you have coyotes in the area, you will need to use two 18" stakes and swivels for each trap you set. And last but not least, you need a spray bottle and one gallon of propylene glycol for freeze-proofing your set.

Just starting out you will not need many hide stretchers. Start with a minimum of 1 - dozen muskrat stretchers, 3 mink stretchers, three weasel stretchers (if you're trapping weasel), and depending on your area, 6 - 12 coon and fox stretchers. For larger animals, you'll need three coyote stretchers and a couple of ¾" plywood boards set up for beaver. A good fleshing knife is a must (I recommend the Necker-600). And finally, a fleshing beam and skinning knife. The best skinning knife I have ever used is the Frost Mora with a stainless-steel blade. It's awesome steel that you can re-sharpen easily and they hold an edge for a good while. You may also be able to get some used chicken butchering knives for a few dollars each at local flea markets. I bought ten of those when I had the chance, so I have a stack of sharp knives to keep skinning the entire days catch without having to stop to sharpen my knife. You'll also need a small thin bladed knife for smaller animals.

For the beginner, conibears will get you into fur quicker than any other method. Snares are next best, followed by leg restraining traps, and then cage type traps. Not long ago, I helped a young man in Texas get started with trapping. I started him out running six #220 conibears, and he was able to trap 44 coons in his first month! Now, to be fair, he was trapping in a really good coon area. So, you have to figure out what the most plentiful animal in your area is and then gear up for it.

Each trap or snare has its own unique purpose. I have learned over the years to lean heavily toward snares for survival, because they are light weight and easy to carry, easy to secure to a tree, and fairly low cost. Consider this: 1 - dozen #330 conibears weigh almost 50 pounds, and cost around $240. While, 1 - dozen medium game snares cost $18.99, and weigh in at around four pounds. They will both do a good job of securing meat for you, but why lug around 50 pounds when you don't have to? Another reason snares are so great is that they don't require freeze-proofing. You just need to make sure you set them under cover to keep the snow and freezing rain off of them.

The #110 conibear is the best small game trap to own and use; it's just that simple. Why is that? Because of the simple fact that one of them weighs 12 ounces, and can be folded up to fit in a jacket pocket. And, you don't need to carry around any extra tools to set them with. You can cut off the chain and replace it with 36" of #14 gauge wire, speed dip it with the wire on, and you are set to trap. How simple is that?

Another way to freeze proof your leg restraining traps is to use cattail duff. That's the little brown part everyone tries to make torches out of in the fall or winter. You can collect three or four of these and puff them out, removing the duff from the stem, and bed your trap in that Then cover the top of the trap with just a little bit of duff, followed by just enough dirt to hold the duff over the trap. You don't want to completely cover the duff with dirt, just enough to keep the wind from blowing it clear.

Getting Ready for Trapping Season

I was going through my trapping equipment the other day checking and cleaning the traps up. I do this often. On the conibears, I always check them to make sure my trap tag is still secure. Most states require a trap tag on traps with your name and address on them, so be sure to check your local trapping regulations. I check the safety catches and set the trap, then fire it to make sure all is in working order. Sometimes, on the larger #330 conibears, the eye opens a little during normal use. If the eye opens too much, then the jaws can pop out. If they are open a little, I just whack them closed with a hammer. Then, if the trap checks out, I place them in the dye pile. If I can't fix them quickly, I put those traps in the 'to be repaired' pile. I have hundreds of traps to check, so this can take a lot of time.

The fox and coyote leg hold traps take more time than all the others combined. I clean them up, set the trap and test fire them with a 2 - ½ pound lifting weight. First, I place a 1-pound hammer on the center of the pan. The trap should not fire on the hammer. If it does, I tighten the adjustment screw and try again. Once it will support the hammer then I try the 2 1/2-pound weight. The trap should fire crisp and smooth. I bought some used traps a few years back and as I tested them with a weight, some fired at 6 pounds and some fired at 8 ounces. And those all came from the same pile. I always test the pan on my traps because 'good enough' is not an option for me. Nothing in the world is more frustrating than seeing fox tracks on the dirt on top of the trap pan. That means the trap didn't fire and you missed the fox. Yes, it has happened to me.

Next, I check the trap chain and look for any weak spots. I also make sure the trap tag is secure. Next, I make sure all the swivels are working correctly. Sometimes, a coyote will chew up a swivel so bad it has to be replaced. Then I set the trap and make sure the pan is level with the top of the base plate. All of my leg-hold traps are laminated. What that means is that I welded #9 wire on the top outside of the jaws of the trap, in order to increase the size of the jaws. This little trick gives the jaws more surface area and therefore, more clamping/holding power on the animal's leg. I always check to make sure the welds aren't cracked and are still in good shape. Once that's done, I put that trap in the dye pile and move on to the next.

The type and condition of your equipment will directly affect your success in trapping. If you buy a pile of old used traps that have not been stored properly, the springs on the coil spring traps will most likely be weak and in need of replacing. I would put them in the pile of traps to be worked on, because if there's a lot of rust on them I know they will always need a lot of work. I bought a pile like that a few years back for muskrat trapping. After going through them, 2 out of 12 failed to meet my standards. What was wrong with them? They had weak rusted chains that could easily be broken by an animal. And they were missing trap pans, so the trap could not even be set. There were weak springs that would not close fast. Also, the jaws were misaligned so that when the trap closed, the jaws weren't even. This will cause pullouts because the trap needs both surfaces of the jaws to close and hold together evenly in order for the full strength of the trap to hold the animal.

 On new traps you need to remove the factory grease before you do anything else. This is easy to do in warm water with Dawn dish soap. The soap easily breaks off the grease and oil. Rinse the trap in hot water ensuring no trace of the dish soap can be smelled. Whether working with conibears or legholds, toss them outside and in 7-10 days the traps will have a light coating of rust. Set and fire the trap knocking off the rust. If you're using leg restraining traps you should have already laminated them at this point. Take a file and file the end of the dog and the pan notch square. This ensures the trap is ready to set. Make sure when you're trap is set the trap pan is level with the center post. To adjust, tap on the Dog arm with hammer to bring it closer or use visegrip to pull it out further. Takes some

practice to do it right. New legholds can sometimes be slow to rust. So take 100 grit emery cloth and scuff up the trap on the pan jaws and spring levers. Once the trap is rusted then you are ready to dye and wax.

This #3 Bridger is dyed, waxed and ready for action.

Good equipment will catch more animals. It's just that simple. For that reason, you can't go wrong buying conibears. They are so nice to use and work with and need very few adjustments right from the factory. The springs are high quality steel and stay strong for years. All you have to do is set the trap, and once the animal sticks his head in, he's yours. Once in awhile you'll find a conibear set off with nothing in it. Sometimes, it's a do-gooder setting the trap off just to mess you up. Sometimes, the animal is carrying a stick and trips the trap. Or, sometimes it's a trap shy animal that set it off. I look the area over and try to determine why it happened, and 99% of the time, I move the trap to a new location.

Now, when you're ready to dye your fox and coyote traps, make sure they're clean, as being clean should be foremost in your mind. I boil my traps in plain water to remove all the junk from last year. Then I pour the water off and rinse the traps in hot water. Finally, I hang them up in a tree and allow them to air out for a few days. Then I pour some trap dye in the pot and bring the dye to a low boil. The first thing I do is clean my

Rubber Made Rough Necks that I store my traps in. I have already washed them and rinsed them three times in hot water, and allowed them to air dry for a few days. Now, I take about a pint of hot dye and splash it in and put the lid on and shake it up so that the logwood scent is all over the inside. I dump that outside. Now, that storage container is ready to store traps. So, I seal the top on and store it outside.

I simmer the traps for 30 minutes and I have them all wired together, so I can just lift the wire up and haul the traps up and out of the pot I am boiling them in. I then allow them to dry by hanging on the outside of my porch. I get another batch going in the pot and then get the trap wax melted in a different pot. When the first traps are dry I set them in the hot wax and let them set a minute and slowly pull them out of the wax. You only want a thin light coat of wax. Make sure you are wearing gloves for everything you have handled with your hands. Clean rubber gloves work best for this.

Hang the traps in a tree for a few days, then store in the Rubber Made containers. It's best to do the waxing part outside. When you pull the traps up out of the melted wax, shake off the excess so you have a nice even coat. Some people melt the wax on top of the dye. Some have just a wax pot. Whatever way you decide, make sure you are thinking safety first. Wax will catch on fire with the right conditions. If it starts smoking, your heat is too hot. Make sure you keep the kids back from this hot wax because melted wax will cause very severe burns. Be careful and have a cotton duck tarp standing by to smother any flames. Wax is made from petroleum so using water on this type of fire will only spread the fire. THINK SAFETY FIRST!

So, you have your traps ready and the wife is ready to kill you for the mess in her kitchen. Now is the time to go scouting. By the time you get back, the wife may have calmed down. Maybe you should make it an overnight camping trip if it's a real mess. It's good practice anyway, so grab your gear and go camping. Some women get upset with me after I get their husband into trapping. Just because the house smells like the woods. What kind of woman would be upset with the refreshing smell of logwood dye is beyond me. Wait, maybe it's when the guy starts late season predator trapping. Oh, the wonderful smell of long-distance fox lure that has a skunk base. OOPS, sorry guys, I shouldn't have told the women.

One friend of mine came up with this brilliant idea for washing his traps. He wanted them sparkling clean before he dyed them. Let's think about this one for a minute. Hmmm… sparkling clean; oh yea, that's a TV commercial. What was the name of that dishwashing soap? Oh, how did you guess, he placed his traps in the dishwasher. There was skunk smell, wax, dye, dirt, leaves, grass and other assorted junk all over the inside of the dishwasher. Can you believe that? I must admit it did do a pretty fair job on the traps though. We had to dye them at my house that year for some reason. I don't remember when his wife started talking to me again. I think it was a few years after that. Something about it being all your fault, if he'd never met you this wouldn't have happened! Or something like that. I think that was what she was yelling at me when we loaded the truck with traps. Women!

I was too excited about trapping season to let a little thing like a dirty dishwasher bother me. Besides, since it was dirty I thought we should do all the traps that way. Why clean it twice? For some reason the husband wouldn't let me ask her if I could do my traps in her dishwasher. She'll get over it. Besides, we're going to get piles of fur this year so when she sees that fur check all will be forgiven. Well, in 3 months that is, when the first fur check arrives. Hey friend, my basement has a little room, you can sleep there for a few nights.

Chapter 3: Making Your Equipment the Best

Ok, we all want the best equipment money can buy. But traps and snares are mass produced and need to be fine-tuned by you, the trapper. This is what separates the pro's from the amateurs. There is no such thing as 'good enough' when it comes to traps and snares. Either it works right or it's junk. You should never ever set a faulty trap because it can and will cost you fur and at the same time will educate the animals. Let's start with an easy one - preparing conibears.

When you buy conibears new, they come coated with oil and grease from the factory. Now most hunters want oil on their guns because it stops them from rusting. But, you have to change how you think about metal and rust when it comes to traps and snares. Traps aren't guns, so forget about using gun blue on traps and all the other neat tricks you hear about and do it right. First thing you do is wash the trap off in hot water with Dawn dish soap or any brand that has grease cutter in it. Rinse in hot water real good and make sure every tiny bit of the dish soap is rinsed off. Now if you are married (warning warning Will Robinson) do not do this in the kitchen sink unless you plan to clean up all the grease before your wife catches you (grin). Some women have no sense of humor. Next, toss the traps outside and allow them to get rusty. If you're in a dry climate like the southwest, you might have to water them every day for a week.

Once they get a fine coat of rust on them set the traps and fire them a few times to knock off the lose rust. The only adjustment on conibears you can make is the top three-prong trigger on the #110 or two-prong trigger on the rest. What you want to happen when an animal hits the trigger is for the trigger to only move about 1/4 of an inch before it fires. You can adjust this by taking a rat tail file and filing the notch a little deeper so the trigger part hits quicker.

Now, you're ready to speed dip. Follow the directions on the can and dip the traps. Allow to air dry over night then dip them again the next day and if you want a thorough job, dip them a third time and allow to air dry for 2 weeks before using. I prefer do this in the spring 4 months before using. Next, work the two-prong trigger free because the dip may glue it in place. You may have to put 1 or 2 drops of WD-40 inside, on the trigger notch.

Just a little is all it takes. Now work the trigger back and forth until it's loose and fast. Wipe off all WD-40 or it will remove the speed dip. Once they are aired out store in Rubber made totes until you're ready to use them. Before you store them, set them again and be sure to wear gloves because you will get some speed dip on your hands otherwise. Set and fire on a stick and make sure they are working correctly. Seems pretty simple, wouldn't you say? Now you don't have to speed dip again until you see rust on them. Sometimes as long as 2 - 3 years later.

Snares are a different story. The first thing you need to do is unwrap the snares and single wrap each one. Make the loop opening the size you want to use. As an example, let's say you want a Coon size; you make an 8 inch loop and then wrap the rest of the snare around the loop. Now you need to season them. Use a pot large enough to hold all the snares coiled up. Fill the pot with water and bring the water to a boil. Then lower the heat and carefully add 1 cup of baking soda. Add it slowly, as the water can boil over while adding the baking soda. Put your snares in the water, set the fire for a light boil, and leave them in for 5 minutes. Then remove the snares and rinse them thoroughly in hot water (be careful with the boiling water and hot snares). Now, rinse the snares thoroughly to remove any trace of baking soda and put them outside and allow them to weather for 1 - 2 weeks. The snares should appear light grey when finished.

If you're going to store them for a long time, it would be a good idea to melt some wax and dip the swivel and lock to stop them from rusting too much. Heat water in a pan but don't bring it to a boil. Then melt canning wax on top of the water. Dip snare parts in and slowly pull them up through the melted wax. You will get some on the cable but that's no big deal. If you plan on using them within in a year or so, there's no need to wax them. Be very careful when working with melted wax. Do not do this near an open flame.

Now you need to form the snare to work for you. Some people call this loading the snare. I call it working the snare. There may be little flaws in the snares on the locks and cable. Your goal is to get the snare to close smoothly and quickly. First, you open the snare to the size of animal you want to catch. Let's say you want a rabbit sized loop. Make the loop 5 inches. Hold the snare cable behind the loop with your right hand and grab the lock with your left hand. Cock the lock by holding the top part with the fingers and thumb of your left hand. Hold the bottom with your right hand and pull the lock closed. Do this several times as this will clear off the burrs you can't see and you will feel the lock get smoother and close faster when you test it. Now the snare loop will look like a teardrop shape and what you want is more of a rounded look. Open the snare to the desired size and while holding the lock with one hand about halfway down from the lock at the 9 o'clock position bend it gently to give it a set. Not real hard or you'll kink the cable. Now do the same at the three o'clock position. This will give the snare a more rounded shape. This is hard to explain but play with the snare and you'll get a feel for it.

Tear Drop snare

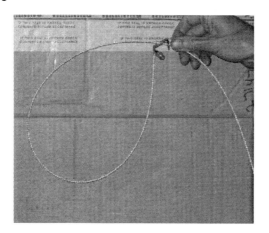

Work the snare while holding it like this, and pull it closed, making the cable smooth.

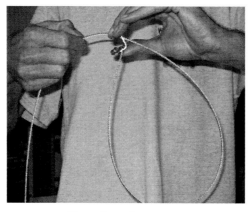

Forming the snare.

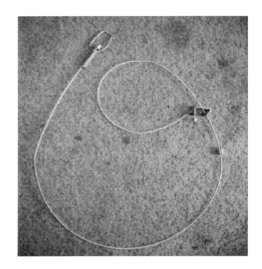

A rounder snare is smoother and faster.

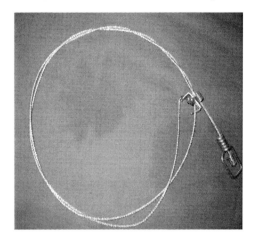

Ready to boil in baking soda.

After you boil the snares, let the weather work them one more time and test them to make sure they close fast. Now you store them at the size you want. This will help to put memory in the cable for the more rounded look.

Waxing and Dyeing Traps

First off, I would like to thank all the wonderful people that have e-mailed me. All your questions and comments have helped me. Two comments that have come up were about waxing traps and homemade dyes for traps. DO NOT WAX CONIBEARS.

Please listen to me, the main reason you wax traps is to preserve the traps and to make them lighting fast. This is something you want when you're trapping predators on land when the traps are possibly buried under ground for weeks at a time. The wax is very good to have on the traps then. Waxing water leg-hold traps poses two problems. The first is, the wax makes the jaws of the traps slippery and a large powerful coon can pull his foot out. Second, on bright moonlit nights, the wax is shiny and sometimes a coon will grab the jaw of the trap, setting it off without getting caught.

Raccoons are very curious animals and they just love to grab shiny things in the water. One of the oldest methods of trapping coons is to wrap the pan of a leg-hold with tin foil. The coon will see the shiny foil and grab the pan, setting the trap off on his paw. But, if they grab the outside jaw of the trap, the trap will fire without the coon getting caught. The biggest reason you don't want to wax conibears is they become so touchy that sometimes while you are setting them they will fire off spraying you with water. Or, if you're unlucky, they'll fire off and whack your hand. This safety reason is why I didn't even mention it. I waxed conibears one year and had traps firing off in the water as I tried to set them; I swore I would never wax conibears again. And I haven't, and neither should you.

Please, for your own safety, don't wax conibears. For you folks that are new to trapping, waxing traps was considered the only way to go years ago. The reason waxing is good for land traps is that the wax makes the trap faster and it comes up through the ground better. It also preserves the trap and keeps it from rusting. If you are land trapping with leg-holds, this method is still recommended. There is no reason to wax your conibears or your water leg-holds. Do not wax conibears. Did I mention that you should not wax conibears?

Homemade Trap Dye

The following information was sent to me from one reader that preferred this method of dyeing traps. I would like to thank Blue Skies for sending this to me.

Collect black walnut hulls in the early fall when the hulls are starting to separate from the nut. Collect about a gallon, and put them in a 5-gallon pot filled with water and boil them for at least

30 minutes. Wire your traps together and lower them into the pot. Remove the pot from the fire and when it has cooled down, put it outside. Two days later, remove the traps from the pot and hang them in a tree to air dry. Once they're dry, pack them in a clean box until you're ready to start trapping.

A warning from Blue Skies: Don't get any dye on your hands or you'll wear it for a week because you can't wash it off. That's why you wire the traps together and leave some wire hanging out of the pot. Then, you can just grab the wire and pull the traps out when they're done.

This is a good natural dye and scent for your traps. Another good one is stag horn sumac berries. Do the same process as described above. I have found that if you are just hobby trapping, a few traps here and there for a couple of weeks each year, that's all you'll need. You still need to degrease and rust your traps first, as described before. The old thinking was that if you used natural dyes you would catch more animals. I have caught too many animals next to rusting farm equipment not to be convinced that rust doesn't scare animals. But in a survival situation, it's good to know how to make natural dyes to keep your traps in top working order.

Trapping is a lot like politics; some people are convinced certain ways are the best, and others believe different. I go by what works for me. Natural homemade dyes are just one more method to dye your traps that will help you get twenty years use out of the equipment. So please try this method if you know where there are some walnut trees.

Why Conibears?

The question 'why conibears?", also came up in a recent e-mail, and I thought I would share my knowledge with you. Recommending traps is just a logical, or educated guess on my part. I look at what a beginner would have the most success with and think about which animals are the most plentiful to trap for. Muskrats, beavers and raccoons are just about everywhere in the U.S., and all three are fairly easy to trap. And I feel that just about anyone can catch critters with conibears. You see, I was thinking long term, and wanted to recommend the most reliable way people could prepare and actually catch fur and meat to provide for their families.

Conibears are the best traps for beginners because:
- There is no trap adjustment.
- All you need to carry is wire and pliers since no stakes are needed, which means you won't have to lug a hammer around with you.
- Once the animal is caught, it's usually dead within 4 to 6 minutes.
- The concept is easy to understand. The animal is trying to go through the trap.
- Snares can get knocked over, but a well-stabilized conibear will not.
- A leg-hold trap on land must be buried. This causes you to carry a sifter and anti-freeze.
- Conibears are less of a theft problem, because a dead animal is harder to spot than a live one.
- Snares and leg-holds need to be staked or grappled and conibears don't. Again, less equipment to carry.

The disadvantages

- You must use care and caution and pay special attention when setting to avoid catching dogs and cats.
- You will not catch many fox and coyotes with them.
- You must use care and caution when setting, because these traps hurt more than leg-holds if you get hit with one on the hand.
- Some trap-shy animals will walk or swim by without going in the trap.

I hope you enjoyed this section of the book and decide to go out and try it for yourself. It's a lot of fun. There's just no better feeling in the world than knowing that if there are muskrats, beavers and raccoons around you know you can eat. It's good to know that with just a dozen traps, you're home free.

Using Scent and Lures

The issue of human scent has come up a few times over the years. When you are trapping, you have to minimize human scent. The first thing you have to do is make sure your equipment is clean and as scent-free as possible. After that, your boots leave behind the most human scent. So while you are in trapping mode, you don't want to go into a gas station and walk around there in the same boots you plan to wear for trapping. Think about the last time you were at a gas station. Did you see spilled gas, anti-freeze, oil spots, etc… on the ground? Even if it appears clean, all those different smells are all around you, so just by walking there, you are picking up foreign smells that will warn animals of your presence. So don't wear your trapping boots when you gas up.

Here is an example of how important human scent is on the fox trapping line. As a trapper, I run my own traps, and every year a friend and his son would come trapping with me for one day. The young boy had a ball and loved seeing the foxes and raccoons. I really enjoy having them come along. After three years of doing this, I noticed a pattern. The next day after all three of us had checked the traps; the catch would drop way off. Why? Because of all the extra human scent around the sets. So, if you take someone with you when you are trapping, you are going to catch less than if you trap by yourself. That applies mainly to land trapping.

When you are land trapping foxes and coyotes, you should keep your vehicle clean and walk in mud puddles to wash the scent off your boots. Check your traps from a distance with binoculars in order to stay away form your sets. Always be aware of your scent and try your best to keep it at a minimum. The foxes and coyotes will still know you've been there, but you don't want them to know you're there every day. Use binoculars so you can check your traps from a distance and keep from spreading your scent around the trap site.

Water trapping is different. Since you are wearing hip boots or waders, your scent is not a problem because the water keeps them clean. The only pattern I have seen with water trapping as regards scent is that if you have more than one person with you and you are yelling back and forth a lot, the catch drops the next day. So you need to realize that your behavior can also impact your catch. Just keep that in mind. I have trapped plenty of raccoons and beaver while setting the trap bare handed, even though I know better. You should always use gloves, so just get in the habit of wearing clean, scent-free gloves any time you touch your traps. Store the gloves in the same container you keep your traps in just to make it easy on yourself. Always wash your hands and then rub them with fresh dirt or leaves before handling the gloves or trap containers.

There was a question about rust that came up concerning coyote trapping that I would like to cover here. My answer is simple: stop and think about all the barbed wire fences in America, and realize that a coyote's feeding range can be as far as 50 miles from his home base. Inside those 50 miles, how many barbed wire fences do you suppose he's gone under? When setting coyote traps, if a little rust appears on the trap, spray fox or coyote urine over the trap cover. This will show the next coyote that another coyote has already been there and it is safe to walk up. For conibears set in water, scent should not be a problem. Also, when setting the #220 on land, scent is not an issue with coons. Coons have no problem raiding chicken coops or garbage cans and do not fear human scent the same way as a fox or coyote does.

 When I say something about trapping the exclusive ones, that is what I'm talking about - the foxes and coyotes. I think most of you will be trapping with conibears for the first few years, going after muskrats, raccoons, beavers, and easier animals at first. Human scent is not that much of a concern, but having a trap well blended into the environment is a big concern. Like I said earlier, know what your are trapping and don't wear your trapping boots to the gas station when you fuel up. Carry your trapping boots in a clean trash bag or box and wear your regular boots to the gas station.

There is a rule that the old deer hunters use around here. If you wound a deer at just before dark, track him until you find him. All you have to do is touch the deer. Then the deer is safe from coyotes that night and maybe the next night. Now why do you suppose that is true? It's because of trappers and their impact on the coyotes behavior. That's right - coyotes learn that fresh kill with human scent equals danger. So think about it when you're trapping coyotes. Check your traps from a distance using binoculars to keep your scent down and you will catch more animals.

Lures are attractors designed to bring the animal closer and make it curious about your set. Because animals are sometime fussy, use a blended lure that is a mixture of different ingredients. Of all the different ingredients available, it only takes one to make the animal dig. Lure is hard for beginners to understand. It is an attractor, so in order for it to work properly, the animal has to smell it. There are many different things that will determine how much lure to use and when to re-lure. But, the most important thing to consider is which way the wind is blowing. I watch the weather channel to see what the forecast is for the coming week. Let's say for Saturday through Sunday, the wind will be coming from the Northwest. Then on Monday and Tuesday, it will shift to the Southwest, and the rest of the week the winds will again be out of the Northwest. With that forecast in mind, I would make 80% of my sets so the back of the set is facing Northwest and 20% of my sets facing Southwest. So you see, the majority of time for the whole week the wind will be out of the Northwest. That is why I make up 80% of my sets that way. But to prevent me from having two slow days on the trapline, I set 20% of my sets for Monday and Tuesday.

After several years, I discovered that the best way to test fox and coyote lures is to let my dog test them. It only took a few years of that until I settled on one lure supplier for all of my predator lures. I prefer my own lure for the three different types that I make myself.

Lasting Lures

So how do you use lures anyway? You either place 6 - 9 drops of lure on your sets or drop a small lima-bean sized piece of bait (commercially produced) down the hole. How long does it last? That depends on many different things. First off, did you make a catch and the animal ate or dug it up so much it is not working anymore? What I do is re-set the trap and the next day if there is not another catch then I re-lure. Always re-lure after a rain, even if it only rains hard for 10 minutes. My best catch every year is always that one night when it is foggy or misting light rain. Why do you think that is? My theory is that because it is so dark out, the animals hunt more by their nose, and they can't see little things wrong at the set that may otherwise scare them off. Also, it is so dark they have trouble hunting, so they go more for what is already dead. Finally, I think the lure scent carries better in the mist and makes it easier for them to find the set.

Now, if you know this type of weather is coming, you should re-lure that day to make sure you are ready to take advantage of such prime trapping conditions. This is very important. I don't care what you are trapping, make sure you re-lure and all your sets are in good shape. Then go home and sharpen the skinning knife because the next day you are going to be busy.

Cold will also effect how lures work. When the temperature is above 32 degrees, I don't change anything. But when it drops below 32 degrees, I double the amount of lure. Below 0 degrees, I triple the amount of lure. This is for land trapping because when below freezing, you are trapping under the ice and water trapping. In faster moving creeks, streams, and rivers your sets will keep working longer because they don't freeze up like in still water.

After the first season, you should have made enough to pay back your investment on traps. The next year, you can buy more traps and spend more on lures and baits. What good is having traps without good lure? Here is an example about lure that will help you understand what I mean. The guy that tested my beaver lure ran out of it on his very first day. So by the third day, his catch dropped to 20% or less. This guy is one of the top -beaver trappers in the area. So against my better judgment I sold him 4 ounces of my lure. By the end of the week, he was back up to 35 - 50% catch each day. So you see, with lure his catch increased 15 - 30%. What does this equal in real numbers? He was running 40 beaver traps, catching between four and eight beaver a day with no lure. While using lure, his catch jumped to 12 - 20 beaver a day. In terms of money, at an average price of $25 per beaver, his top day of 50% equals $300 more profit. All because of a $12.00 bottle of lure. Now do you see how important lure is? That is just one example. Look at it like this; good lure equals almost guaranteed success. If you use the right lure in the right way, the rest is up to you and your technique.

I have just recently finished my first video on how to trap. With the sets I teach in the video and with a #1 complete package deal, you can make sets for coons like I said earlier. Go get permission and get 24 buckets set out pre-baited, find your muskrat runs and your beaver spots. There is absolutely no reason you cannot catch enough animals to pay for your equipment, give you some extra pocket change and have a freezer full of free meat. Name anything else in your survival supplies that can do that for you. Traps are the only things I know of that actually pay for themselves, provide meat and you will still be able to re-use them every year, over and over again.

.22 Ammo

It never ceases to amaze me how people continually underrate one of the most versatile hunting calibers ever invented: the .22 rimfire cartridge. In the right hands, a good .22 rifle with an assortment of ammo is an extremely effective survival tool. I have shot and killed well over 1,000 animals with .22 ammo, and over the years I have tested all available brands and loads. What I have discovered is simple, but potentially very important for your survival. True hollow-points work best on small and medium sized game. For larger animals, you need a solid point in order to penetrate the skull for a quick, sure kill.

Here's an example for you. Let's say you want to drop a pig in his tracks with a head shot, and you are using good high expansion hollow-points. You blast the pig in the back of the skull and hope he is down for the count. Instead, he runs around screaming and tearing up everything in his path. What went wrong? Well, the back of the skull is the thickest and hardest to penetrate. The hollow-point did what it was supposed to do and flattened out with little penetration. So all you did was make him mad and leave him wounded. If you had used a solid bullet, it would have most likely entered the brain for a quick kill. Choosing the right ammo is like choosing the right tool for the job. You need to know what it can and can't do, and realize that it has definite physical limitations. Also, understanding the anatomy of your prey will help tremendously. Using that same hollow-point ammo, a shot into the ear angled slightly downward, would enter through the ear canal and then the brain. And in that case, the expanding bullet would shred the brain and kill the pig instantly.

The largest coon I ever trapped weighed in at 35 pounds. He was a monster. Needless to say, this coon was not used to losing in a fight. It looked to me like he had won a fight against a coyote because the scars on his hide told the story. Well, he sure wasn't happy to be caught in my trap. Using a catch pole I placed the cable around his neck and locked it down and was taking the foot out of the trap when he popped the cable off his neck and jumped free of the trap.

I had brought along a dog (a 90 pound black-and-tan mixed Lab) that I was trying to train to hunt coons, and he charged in and chased the coon off into the woods. I would like to say the dog won the fight but that would be a big fat lie. That coon put a good whipping on the dog and he backed off. The coon took off running again, the dog treed him in a small tree, and he stopped climbing about 20 feet up. I was using a rifle with Remington yellow jackets. I popped him in the back of the head and he fell out of the tree. But he bounced right back up again and the dog charged in thinking this coon would be dead or dying like other tree shot coons he'd jumped. Nope, this monster fought the dog off again!

Well, that dog looked at me as if he was questioning my marksmanship or something. I shot the coon again and ended the fight. That night when skinning the coon I found the first bullet flatten just under the skin on the back of the skull. I had shot lots of coons with yellow-jackets right in front of the ear and it usually puts them down fast. I learned a valuable lesson that day. Never shoot the back of an animal's skull, because that's the thickets spot for a .22 bullet to try and penetrate.

I met a Canadian trapper that lived in the woods in Canada years ago and only carried a single-shot .22 rifle. He told me that was all he uses to hunt with. He said he'd taken moose, black bears and deer with it. Using solid points aimed right at the eye or right in front of the ear drops even these animals, according to him. He was a great shot and shot all animals in the head, so the solid points work great for him. But, you must understand the part of Canada he was in was very thick and brushy, and a long shot was 35 yards. He grew up this way and had been hunting since he was five years old. For the rest of us that can't shot off hand that good, body shots are more common. This is where the Remington Yellow jacket really shines. Average expansion is comparable to a .36 caliber bullet. More expansion and more energy transferred to the animal results in quicker kills.

The Remington standard hollow-point expands to about .30 caliber and the Winchester hollow-point expands to about .27 cal. In my experience, the worst hollow-points on the market are Federal hollow-points, sold by Wal-Mart. The don't appear to expand at all on impact. What does this mean, in reality, when hunting? The Federal hollow-point will zip through the animal not transferring the energy of the bullet and that will equal more lost game and less for you to eat. I have written this many times. If I was only going to carry a .22, I would have a brick of .22 yellow jackets and 100 rounds of CCI solid points. For small game up to medium game, the Remington hollow-point is awesome for body shots. The solid point would be for penetrating the skulls of larger animals.

Early last spring, I believe it was a 70 some year old woman killed a Mountain Lion with a .22. She had grown up on the farm and understood where to shoot the animal in order to kill it. She aimed right behind the front shoulder where the hide changes to white. That is where the heart sits and one shot dropped the big cat. On the other hand, shooting a deer in the heart or lungs with a .22 will cause many to be wounded and lost. There was also a case in Canada last winter where two wolves attacked a family that was out sledding. The father was able to kill both wolves with a Ruger 10-22. Yes, wolves do attack people. Again, this shows that a .22 is a great weapon once you understand how to use it.

You've probably heard about the CCI Stinger shells. They are good fast ammo, but super loud. And while they do put animals down quickly, they have a habit of tearing up small game too much. Then there's the new ammo from Mexico. I have tried it and found it to be very dirty ammo, which is why I don't use or recommend it.

There was a case in Bosnia a few years back when the ethic cleansing was going on. A woman's house was invaded by ten well-trained troops, intent on raping her. She pulled a .22 pistol out that held 10 rounds and drove them all out of the house. Most people don't recommend a .22 for home defense, but in the hands of a competent shooter, it is just as deadly as any other firearm.

Chapter 4: Dry Land Trapping

Why Leg Hold Traps?

The leg-hold trap has been around for centuries. Thankfully, in the past 40 years, many improvements have been made in the name of animal comfort. Coil spring traps of all kinds were tested and the results will surprise most hunters. The test animals were outfitted with sensors to monitor both their breathing and heart rate. The results were that the animals only fought the trap on average for 15 minutes. After that, the animals began to calm down, and after an hour, their heartbeat and breathing returned to near normal levels. So you see, it's inaccurate to claim that the animal is in pain the whole time. You cannot argue with scientific facts.

At just before daylight, the animal would again fight the trap because this is the normal time for the animal to go to its bedding area and sleep for the day, so after a brief renewed attempt to break free, the captured animal normally curls up and goes to sleep. Therefore, an animal in a trap that is checked every day is not in any great pain. In fact, this same study proved that some forms of hunting with dogs were *more* stressful for the animals than the trap. So to all you hunters out there that have told me over the years you could "never trap and cause that much pain to an animal", you are living in a dream world.

I have talked to many people over the years and have met the armchair experts who have caught "a few" animals. They talk to one or two trappers and think they have the big picture. I talked to one guy who was the typical know-it-all. He had met a professional water trapper down south years ago. I told him that "back in the fur days" there were professional fox and coyote trappers. He responded in a loud voice "that's BS, no one could trap enough fox to make a living at it". I have met the pros and was trained by one that is still making his living to this day trapping predators:

You wouldn't ask a movie star to fix your car, so don't listen to hunters about trapping. It is a completely different thing. Don't get me wrong, I'm not bashing hunters. I have hunted for more years than I have trapped. I just want to bring out the facts. Talk is cheap, while results will show you the truth of the matter. You can't skin excuses. Trapping is about having a good knowledge base and working hard. I thought I would get this out in the open, before we discuss the sets for legholds. Man, as a meat and fur harvester, needs to respect the animal enough to do what he can to prevent injuries and suffering. If you choose to, you can modify your traps to be even more humane by doing the following:

1. Weld # 9 wire to the top jaws of your traps. This increases the jaw spread and lessens the "pinch" on the animal's foot.
2. Offset the jaw by welding a ¼" lug on the inside top of the jaws. This will give the animal a ¼-inch gap, allowing blood to flow to the paw.
3. Add two swivels to the trap and an inline shock absorber spring.

Taking these added steps will produce one of the most humane traps in the world. While some animals will still be injured, the chances of that happening are 1 in 100. It is also vital that you check your traps every day. If you don't have the time to tend your traps properly then you shouldn't be trapping. Some hobby trappers only trap on weekends: They set their traps on Friday, check them Saturday and pull them after a final check on

Sunday. This is an excellent example of modifying your process to maintain your professionalism. Whatever you do, make sure you are out checking traps every day they are set.

The best all around set for most predators is the dirt hole set. I have trapped raccoons, possum, skunks, red fox, gray fox, coyotes, bobcats, and mink using this method and it is one of the best all time fur producers.

To make the set you need:

- A #1½ coil spring or larger trap - up to a #3 coil spring if there are coyotes in the area.
- A stake swivel and a stake of ½" rebar with a washer welded on top. The washer has to be welded on top so the stake swivel can spin all the way around the trap. The rebar stake should be 18" to 36" long; I usually use a 24-inch stake.
- A trowel for digging the hole
- A sifter for the dirt-to keep rocks out of the trap area
- A hammer
- Bait and lure
- And a pan cover (I use a steel metal screen).

Dig the hole at a 45-degree angle, 10" to 12" deep and put the dirt from the hole into the sifter. Dig a trap bed in front of your hole, stake the trap, place your pan cover on and bed the trap. Sift dirt over the trap until all is level. The pan's center should be 8 inches from the hole, dead center. Add bait and lure inside the hole and cover with grass.

After a catch - this is very important - shoot the animal in the head with a .22 short and immediately remove the animal 30 feet away from your set. This is so it bleeds well away from the trap area. Clean up the blood with your trowel and toss it away from the area. Scrub the trap down with a tuft of grass to remove any blood or hair and then re-make the set; but this time use all the torn up grass and weeds and form a 'V' with the beginning of the 'V' at the hole, widening out to the back. This will help guide the next animal in over the trap. The area is all "scented up" and any fox in the area will come over to see why all the smell is there. Scented tufts of grass works because basically, animals are lazy. Why go hunt and kill an animal to eat, when there is food available that is free for the taking?

For fox, the location of the set is very important. Set where a dirt road enters a field, where two different crops change or where a drainage ditch runs along a field. Remember the wind; the back of the hole should always be facing the wind so the wind blows the scent over the trap. Most animals approach a trap set from the downwind side; that is why it is vital for you to pay attention to the wind direction.

Leghold traps can also be used on trail sets. One good place is where you see trails entering the field from the woods. Follow the trail for a short distance, looking for a narrowed down spot. Use a small tree, a branch they are stepping over, or a bush they duck under. Look for something that naturally narrows the path down. Dig a trap bed, set the trap, and then stake it. Sift dirt over it as with the dirt hole set, making the area look as it did before you set the trap. Place a 'stepping stick' on both sides of the trap. A one-inch diameter stick will work the best for this; the animal will step over the stick-right into the trap. This is a good set for smart raccoons.

Leg hold traps also work well for a smart beaver, but you'll need a #3 or larger trap. Use a drowner, two stakes and wire. Stake out in deep water. Now, a beaver naturally swims with his front paws tucked up against his body. When his chest hits the bank, he sticks out his foot to walk. So, in order to catch him you need to use a poke stick. Find a spot where the beaver are coming out of the water and dig a trap bed on the bank. Place one stake in deep water and run wire up to the top stake, then place the drowner on the wire. Make sure it only goes down and not up. Set the trap and wiggle it in the mud so that it is solid. Place a small poke stick out from the trap with about 2" to 3" sticking out. Place the lure 18" back, off center from the trap pan, about 8". Beavers have a wide body. The beaver will smell the lure and swim over to see what is going on. They will hit the poke sticks and place their foot out into the trap to climb up. The trap will fire and the beaver will be caught by the front leg. The beaver will dive for deep water and the drowner will hold him on the bottom. After 6 - 12 minutes, the beaver will have drowned.

This set works well where the beaver are trap shy of the #330 Conibear. When you are water trapping any type of animal, set up the trap on a drowner. If you get some swivels, cut off the trap ring on your leg-holds and add the swivel. The swivel is designed to accept a ½" rebar stake. If you are water trapping you now have a built-in drowner. This will help you keep your traps working all the time. If you are having trouble with theft in the area, you can trap on the edge of a field and use two stakes. Run enough wire so the animal can get in cover. That way you can make a set out in the open and let the animal hide itself. You can also use drags. The only problem with a drag is, if the farmer's dog gets caught, he will wander home on the road, dragging the trap with your identification tag on it. If someone sees him, they may try to remove the trap and will usually wind up keeping the trap.

I support hunters, and I believe hunters should always support trappers. It is a proven fact that trappers help with conservation of game animals. So if you want more game to hunt, then you need trappers to help keep the predators in check.

The true art of trapping comes from using leg-restraining traps. This trap, when used on dry land, is what separates the amateur from the true trapper. Understanding how to use this art form is very important, because you will occasionally (accidentally) catch a dog while trapping. And since you're responsible for your actions, it is imperative that you know the proper way to release them unharmed and alive. Another advantage to leg-restraining traps; animals that are shy of conibears and snares can be taken using them. That gives you an extra edge, so you can cover all of your bases.

The basics for using the dry land set are the same, no matter what you are trapping. Pick a spot with nice location and good backing. Always try to keep the wind in your face when choosing a trap site. The purpose of the backing is to keep the animal from approaching the back side of the set. Now let's take an in-depth look at the dirt hole set.

Making the dirt hole set

There are a hundred different ways to make the set, so we will cover the basic set-up.

1. Pay attention to the wind. The wind should come from the back of the set, so when you are making the set the wind should be in your face. Did I mention the wind? I cannot stress this enough. You can make the perfect set, have the world's best lure and bait, and have fox walk right by your set. If they can't smell it, they won't work it unless they just happen to see it while walking by. An inexperienced trapper will see tracks near their set and think the lure or bait is useless, never stopping to think which way the wind was coming from last night. You have to think about this stuff!

2. Choose a backing. This can be anything; a large rock, a steep bank, a stump, a log or a piece of firewood. The spot pictured here is ideal for a dirt hole set. You need something to block the back side of the set and force the animal to come around to the front.

3. Dig a hole at a 45 - 80 degree angle, 12-18 inches deep

4. Spread the dirt out behind the hole in an oval shape

5. Dig a trap bed and clear out a space just the size of the trap. Make sure that when you're done, you cover it with dirt so the trap pan is the lowest spot in front of the hole. Read that part again. The trap pan, when finished, must be the lowest spot in front of the hole. It is very important that you understand that. You will hear new trappers talk about the fox stepping all around the hole but never hitting the trap pan. I can almost guarantee the problem is the trap pan was the *highest* spot and the fox stepped around it. This is a canine trait that always holds true.

6. Set the trap and place the pan cover. Place the trap in front of the hole. The top part of the jaw should touch the edge of the hole. The trap needs to be cocked at a 45-degree angle. I'm right handed, so I normally cock it to the right. Why cock it? This puts the trap dog to one side, giving the trap pan the most area to cover. The end result is more fox in the traps. What is a pan cover, you ask? The job of the pan cover is to keep dirt from getting under the trap pan and prevent the trap from firing. There are many different types of pan covers. Steel wire screen (the kind that rusts, never use galvanized or stainless). Wax paper is a good choice. Use a hamburger wax paper cover or cut your own wax paper. The latex covers on the market are a waste of money. I had really bad luck with them. A foam cushion under the pan is ok, but I prefer a pan cover. Even wadded up grass under the trap will work. This is in the early season. During really cold weather, you want to place wax paper on the bottom of the trap bed and wax paper on the trap pan cover and use propylene glycol or waxed dirt. In extremely cold weather, it's much more effective to switch to snares than to fight the frozen ground and run out of dry dirt.

7. Pound the trap stake so the loose jaw will rest on top of it. This will help firm up the trap. If you don't have coyotes in the area, a single 24-inch long ½" diameter length of rebar makes the best stake. If you do have coyotes in the area, you'll want double stakes. Switch to double stake swivels and 18" X ½" rebar. Pound it in so that if forms an 'X'. This is also great for preventing trap thieves from stealing your trap. You would be surprised at who will steal your traps; hunters, farmers, other trappers and sometimes the moron animal rights people.

8. "Bed the trap." Huh? I can't count the number of times I have taken students out and had them make a dirt hole set and they didn't listen to me about bedding traps. A poorly bedded trap equals a dug up trap or missed catches. Do it right the first time. When you first start out, if it takes you all day to set 12 traps, so be it. You are learning do it right the first time. Bedding the trap means that you can touch any part of the trap and it will not move or shift. I normally test the loose jaw to see if the trap will move by placing my finger on it and pushing down. If the trap moves at all, keep pounding dirt around the outside of the whole trap until it doesn't move.

9. Sift dirt over the trap.
Once the trap is firmly in the ground, sift ¼" to ½" of dirt over the top of it. Use your trapper trowel to move just a little bit of dirt off the center of the trap pan so it is the lowest spot in front of the trap. Use a stick to protect the dog. Add clumps of dirt or rocks in front and to the sides to line the animal up with the trap pan. Make sure no rocks or hard dirt clumps are inside the trap set. Once you get freezing conditions, you will want to use wax paper pan covers and propylene glycol as an anti-freeze on the

sifted dirt, spraying about 1 - 2 oz. into the dirt. This prevents it from freezing.

The finished set

10. Add bait and lure. Make sure no part of the lure or bait touches or falls into the trap bed. Why? Because this could cause the animal to dig there, exposing the trap. You don't want the animal to dig, you want them to step on the trap pan.

11. Brush away all human sign from the dirt. This should be self-explanatory.

Got the rabbit killer.

Equipment you will need.

- A bucket to carry everything in, with an outside lure pouch.
- A trapper's hammer
- A trapper's trowel
- A dirt sifter
- Trap stakes

- Pan covers
- Clean leather or rubber gloves that are only used for trapping.

Listen well, because this knowledge was gleaned from past customer mistakes. Why do coyotes and foxes keep digging up your sets? This is the hardest question to answer, because I'm not there to see what you're doing wrong. Common mistakes are as follows:

1. The number 1 problem is improperly bedded traps. Pound and pack the dirt solid all around the trap. You test by putting you finger on the jaw of the trap if it wiggles, moves, shifts, settles or does anything but stay solid, keep bedding the trap.

2. Spilling bait or lure in the trap bed.
3. Containment traps. You have them stored next to a gas can for example. You have to re-boil and wax your traps.

4. You were not paying attention to the wind and the animal works the set from the side or the back.

I once had a trap shy fox that drove me crazy. Any new set I put in she would dig up. It was like a game for her. She would dig the edge of the trap enough to expose about 2 inches of the trap pan and the loose jaw. She thought it was funny as heck I am sure. It was like she ran around and uncovered all my traps first thing every night and warned the other foxes to stay away. Now you should be wondering about now why I say it was a she fox. Because I finally caught her. How? Good question.

I watched where she stood in the dirt pattern, and every single time she stood at the back of the set on the right side. I simply added another trap where she was standing. Then I re-cover the original set and spread the dirt over the other new trap too. Next morning she was there waiting in the second trap. A big old female red fox that brought $50 back in 1980. That would be equal $150 in todays dollars.

Another common problem is raccoons that will dig up a lot of traps. And just like the fox in the story above, you can catch them by changing your set from a dirt hole to a flat set, and adding a trap where the animal is most likely to dig the trap up. Just make a new set totally different with different bait 30 feet away. Change, adapt, and overcome.

Coyote Dirt Hole

On a fox dirt hole, you want a 2-3 inch hole. With coyotes you want a 4-6 inch hole.

Note the large hole and large piece of bait that is below the feathers. If it is legal to have a little exposed feathers, it's a great visual attracter.

The trail set shown in the next section will show you my preferred double stake method I use on coyotes. Add double stake swivels and pound the stakes in an "X" shape. This will give your trap set the most strength and holding power. In fact, the double stake method is what they use to hold 100 pound wolves.

Coyotes will fight the trap different than other animal. They can somehow get right over the trap and jump straight in the air and that will pump the stake out of the ground. That is why in coyote territory you always want double stakes. I have tried the new disposable stakes and find them to be more trouble than they are worth. The only place they work really well is in farmers fields. Otherwise, if you get in rocky or rough terrain the disposable stakes will leave you wanting real stakes.

Now on coyote sets, you make the large dirt hole for the best results. You can make really big size holes up to full size shovel sized. Dig it deep, 18-24 inches and use a large piece of bait. You only have a few chances a month on a coyote so make sure you do it right the first time. If you read misinformation saying to use small bait on coyotes ignore that person. You want a large piece of bait about the size of half a muskrat.

How to Make a Trail Set

The trail set is a very good set to learn for taking trap-shy animals. They require no bait, no lure and no urine. Notice the hammer in the center of the trail and the natural stepping stick in the trail.

Use a trowel to cut and remove the sod. Then dig the trap bed and put the soil in sifter. Use a rock to guide the animal into the trap.

This is set for coyotes, so use a double stake in an X and pound into the bottom of the trap bed.

Note that trap stakes are below ground level; that's very important.

Now bed the trap, packing the dirt around the outside edges. It's very important the trap does not rock or wobble.

Finished trail set.

The Flat Set

Pick a spot with good backing wind in your face. Note the small branch 1/2 inch size is great. Dig the trap bed.

Same as trail if coyotes in the area double stake and bed the trap.

Dirt sifted over set. Natural leaves covering on top.

Extra dirt is hauled away and tossed at least 10 feet from set.

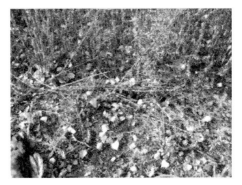

Note how natural the set looks.

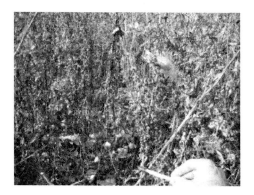

Visual feather set at 3 feet and gland lure placed at 2 feet. The feather can be tied to the plants with a string.

Busted coyote

Trapping different animals

The coyote is a little smarter than the fox, and adapts and changes constantly to meet the challenges of its environment. Their range covers most states and with today's hug a predator attitude, they are even setting up shop right in urban areas all across the United States. Attacks in Arizona and California on children are so numerous, one reporter told me they don't even bother writing the stories anymore because it so commonplace. Why are the attacks so high in those two states? It's most likely because of the trapping ban. The 'hug the predator' crowd banned trapping and now the animals are safe. Too bad the children are not. I read one study that stated that over 78 people had been attacked in California and Arizona. Mostly children and elderly people.

The coyote has a huge hunting area as compared to the fox. His circle is anywhere from three to 14 days in length, with an average of 10 days in most states. What does this mean? If you have coyote traps out, during 30 days of trapping, you have three chances to catch them. That's according to per pack travel patterns. If you are in an area where more than one pack travels, then you might have six chances a month. Coyotes are excellent hunters and do not always come into bait until the weather is cold, the game is scare, and hunger drives them to scavenge more than hunt.

Coyotes are fairly easy to snare. Trapping them and holding them is the secret. Again, good equipment equals success. Coyote will pull a single stake out of the ground when trapped, they fight a trap different than any animal I have seen. They will jump straight up with their hind leg pumping the stake and once they feel it give a little, they'll keep doing it until the stake pops out. That's why I recommend double stakes for coyotes. Disposable stakes are real popular with some trappers, but I have had nothing but trouble with them. In the wrong type of ground, they will not set right, if you hit a rock, they'll jam. The only place I have seen them work well is on farmers field where crops are grown.

Coyotes breed in February and have their pups in April. Much like fox, they have 4-6 pups on the average and sometimes as many as 11. The pack forms and sticks together, but unlike other animals, coyotes are the big coward when one of the pack is killed. They may never return to that farm for months afterward. A smart female may take the pack out of the county. It all depends on the individual coyote. Once trap shy, certain coyotes are almost impossible to trap. The trail set is one way to get the smart ones. Overall, coyotes are much harder to trap with any consistency, than wolves. Do it right the first time and you can take coyotes in good numbers.

One of the best places to trap coyotes is the farmers bone yard. Cows and calves dies every year, and every working farm has a bone yard. Find out where they are. You will have to clean out the skunks, possum and coons first, then they are top spots for trapping the coyotes, especially as the weather turns cold. Once you start trapping and deer season rolls around, I recommend you pull your fox and coyote traps for the first 3 days. Everyone and their cousin is out and I have more fox and coyote traps stolen during this time than any other. I just gave up fighting them because it's not worth the trouble of losing equipment and fur to people who do not have the skill to trap the animal to begin with.

With coyotes, it is best to first check your traps from 50 yards away with binoculars, making sure the trap is not set off. Only approach and inspect the set every 3 days. With coyote trapping, the fewer people you take with you the better. More people equals more scent and fewer coyotes caught for a few days.

The Bridger #2 and 3 are some of the best coyote traps on the market. They have square jaws, high levers, strong springs, and center base swivels. But if I was back east with a lot of people and a lot of dogs, I would use #1-3/4 offset laminated traps. Smaller traps are better for PR.

Bobcats

Bobcat are not real hard to trap but they have a huge hunting circle, taking as much as 1 month to get back to where you last saw them. Seeing fresh bobcat tracks is great when you are scouting but if you are setting traps you may have been too late. Most bobcat are taken in Dirt hole sets and trail sets leading to large bait piles.

Bobcats are very good hunters and may walk right by bait. The #3 coilspring is a very good trap to use on bobcats because of their large feet. In Michigan, I found most of the bobcat hung out at least 1/4 mile off any logging road and would hunt the beaver huts when they came through. My favorite bait was beaver set in large dirt holes or a cubby set.

A cubby set is nothing but a large 18 inch wide by 36 inch long natural brush tunnel you build on the south side of a large tree near an active beaver hut. Cover with 6 inches of Pine boughs. Narrow the front down to 6 inches wide, and that is where you want to set the trap. Toss in 1/4 to 1/2 of a beaver carcass in the back and use some beaver lure. There are several ways to build it using sticks shoved in the ground or large cut pieces of firewood 12 inches thick. Now why did I say on the south side of a tree? Because of Wind and snow. The tree helps to block the snow and keep the trap working longer. Bobcat are powerful animals, so make sure you have good equipment and double stake and you will get them.

Bobcat Trapping up Close

I was running fox traps one year and it was a typical day with a couple of foxes and a few coons in the back of the truck. I pulled up to a farm and walked out to check my set. I was using drags to get away from a theft problem I was having trouble with spotlighters driving around and stealing the animals in my traps. These people are typical in some areas. They usually don't have a job and live on welfare, with kids running wild etc... These type of folks are some of the best poachers in the area. Some areas of the country they call them shiners, spotlighters, jack lighting, and assorted other names. I call them scumbags.

They trespass on private property and drive through the farmers fields, shine deer and shoot them by the truck-full. And, they steal from trappers. As they are out looking for deer with their spotlights, they will come across my foxes, coyotes and coons in traps. While checking my traps, I'll find the trap circle made by an animal and the area looks torn up and an empty trap with a pile of blood where they shot them. You can tell when it's poachers, because they don't steal the traps and they shoot the animal with a .22. Shooting the animal with a shotgun leaves a larger blood spot. The poachers know that the trappers are sick of being stolen from and have marked their traps with welding marks and other tricks. Then the trappers show the game warden, so if the scumbags rip off the trap tag, the trap can still be ID'd in the field. Once the poachers know this, they stop stealing the traps, but not the animals.

I was sick of doing all the work while these leeches were stealing my catch. So, I switched to drags. This works good because the animal goes into bushes and is out of sight and the poachers miss them. Not all, they still find some, but I bring home more fur then when I stake the traps solid. One morning, I came up to farm to check the trap and the drag was gone. It was a cool day, raining lightly, and the woods smelled of fall. A friend of mine was with me and as we looked we noticed a faint trail going into some brush about 20 yards from the trap. I walked in and saw where the area was all torn up. But there was no animal. I looked carefully and could just make out where the animal had pulled through to a dirt road. We spilt up and I allowed the other guy to take the .22 rifle. He took one side of the road about 20 yards in and I took the other side.

The rain had washed away any drag marks away from the surface of the road. About a hundred yards from the set, I heard a noise and saw an animal jumping like mad trying to get out of the trap. At first, because it was so tall and had brownish fur, I thought it was a coyote. Then it  stopped fighting the trap, flattened its ears and let out a blood curdling scream that I will never forget. It was a bobcat and he was only 20 feet away and not afraid of me at all. Considering the circumstances, he decide it was time to fight. Since I didn't have the gun, I decided it was time for some help. I yelled; "bring the gun!" The cat thought this was a challenge (now remember, he is on a drag with 6 feet of chain between me and him) and he charged. I'm yelling; "bring the gun, bring the gun!" The bobcat is snarling and screaming and I'm wondering if the drag is going to pop off. The drag stopped the cat, but he kept growling deeply at me the whole time. My friend came running up and I yelled; "shoot him right now!" The shot ended our standoff quickly. The bobcat weighed in at 31 pounds.

Red Fox

Without a doubt, the red fox is my favorite animal to trap. They're shy, smart, fast, and have a beautiful pelt. Even though coyotes are more challenging to trap, there is just something about red fox that I really enjoy.

Understanding the red fox is the key to successfully trapping them. When most 'civilians' look at a fox, they think they compare in size to a family dog – somewhere in the 20 lb. +/- range. In reality, most foxes weigh somewhere in the 8 -12 pound range. Simple wild canines don't compare to the domestic kind in terms of weight. To begin to try to understand the fox, let's 'follow one' from spring through fall.

A beautiful dark red fox

February – March: The red fox mates during this time. The pair stays together throughout the gestation period; usually about 60 days. The pups (called kits) are born in a ground den; a 10-foot deep hole the fox dug just for this purpose. On average, female foxes will have 4-6 kits per litter. But, I've heard of litters of as many as 10. A good rule of thumb is to expect five on average. The mother stays with them 24/7, and will only leave the den when she needs water. The male will hunt for them both and bring her food. This means the male won't always be around.

When the kits get older and start demanding more food, the female will begin to go hunting and the kits will emerge from the den to play. The fox is a very security conscious animal. The female will have two to three back up dens in the area in case she has to abandon the first den. If she detects a human presence at this stage, she will most likely move the den. Whenever the female hunts, the kits must learn to be on the lookout for predators. Hawks and eagles will often help themselves to the kits at any opportunity. The coyote is the worst enemy the fox has – they'll go out of their way to kill any fox they encounter, including adults and entire litters of kits. The parents establish a hunting area, normally within a 3 - 4 mile range from the den, which they will usually scout once every 24 hours. Depending on where you live, if the food source is not plentiful enough, the fox will sometimes travel in a 2 or 3 day circle. It's hard to talk in general terms because nothing is set in stone. In a good food area for the fox, they prefer to stay within a 1 day hunting circle.

July – August: The kits are now running around getting into trouble like normal children. They practice their hunting skills on mice, voles and even grasshoppers. If berries are in the area, they will eat them as well.

September: By now the kits are almost fully grown. They will start hunting with their parents, who have approximately two months to teach them the hunting and survival skills they'll need for the rest of their lives.

What red foxes hunt – Common food sources

The Delta duck study done in the pothole region of North Dakota showed how effective a hunter the fox truly is. With excellent hearing, exceptional eyesight and lightning fast reflexes, the red fox has been clocked at up to 45 mph; but they can't do that for long. On a short burst, a fox can easily outrun a coyote, but the coyote will outlast them, so the fox learns to find culverts, dens and thick brush piles to protect themselves. Ducks sitting on their nests are a prime target for the fox. The fox will kill and eat the duck and the eggs, or just eat the eggs if the duck happens to escape. Foxes hunt their claimed area every day and some scientists believe they will find eight out of ten duck nests in their area. *In fact, one study preferred coyote over red fox to help ducks increase their hatch rate. The scientists were trying to help increase the duck population so they preferred to see coyotes in the area over red fox.* Why would they recommend coyotes over fox? Common sense tells you that a 25-35 pound coyote would need more food than an 8-12 pound fox. A coyote hunts a huge area; their loop can take them anywhere from three to 14 days to make. Whereas, the red fox will scout the same area every day, day after day.

Ground nesting birds like pheasants, grouse, quail, and song birds are prime targets for the fox. If most hunters truly understood predators, they would be trapping every fall to help balance nature. Rabbits, squirrels, chipmunks, mice, voles and even frogs are hunted and eaten by the fox. In a pinch, they will also eat berries and even fruit on the ground.

Late October - Early November: The parents will now turn on the young and drive them out of 'their' area. Occasionally, one female kit might be allowed to stay, but generally, all the kits are driven from the parents hunting grounds. This is called "The Fall Shuffle" or "Dispersion." *This* is trapping season in most areas, and the fox will be on the move for the next month or so. The kits are now full-grown foxes, and are looking for their own hunting grounds. How do they travel? Ah...now you're asking the right questions.

The kits normally head off into the wind, the females traveling 10 - 40 miles and the males anywhere from 20 to 88 miles. The fox are making a one-way trip, so when they come through your trapping ground you only have one shot at them; because the next day they will be gone. You must also remember these observations are not set in stone. If there is road kill deer or a hunter's 'lost deer', the red fox might hang around for a few days to feed.

As a trapper, you're trying to narrow their world down to a tiny four inches. Think about that for a minute. The fox is traveling, for the sake of this discussion, 30 - 40 miles; you have one and only one shot at them; and you have to narrow where they step down to a four inch area of opportunity. Pretty darn challenging if you ask me. Now the nitty-gritty part is understanding how foxes travel. A fox will normally travel only at night. When they come near a small town they tend to stay about a mile out on the fringe and will search out the first available low spot, ditch, valley or stream to take them around the town. So where do you want to locate your traps? A perfect spot - the one you dream about - is the intersection of a four-lane interstate and a major river.

Here you would have everything in your favor; the river blocks them and forces them to travel along the edge, looking for a way across. A fox coming from another area will hit the interstate and travel along the side, once again, looking for a safe place to cross. You have the perfect travel route, one that narrows into only a very few possibilities. But which side do you set up on?

You have four choices. Ask yourself; "What is the normal wind direction for this time of year?" I usually trap where the wind will be from the Northwest, so the fox is heading into the wind, so your traps should be in the Southeastern corner of the intersection of the interstate and the river.

The good news is that not only fox, but a variety of different animals will travel this corner and you should never pass it up as a set location. Make sure you have ground cover to block the view from the interstate. This can be close to the fence, where the weeds are high enough they will block the view. This works well on most any major waterway or road. Think of a fox as a cat-like dog that loves to travel in low spots but will jump on top of large hay bales to survey his hunting territory. Hay bale stacks are another excellent set location. Why? Because of mice – a favorite food source for fox.

Again - and I will stress this repeatedly - where do you set up? Repeat after me - wind direction, wind direction, wind direction. When the wind is coming from the Northwest, you set up on the Southeast corner. And make sure you ask the farmer or rancher when he plans on moving the bales. I have had more traps ruined by tractors than I would care to admit to.

If there is a pond with any type of drainage (or even a lowland area) heading to it, this is the route the fox will take to the pond. Where do you set up? The best place would be on the southeast side. But remember, the wind will shift, so you'll want a few traps per farm set up on the Northwest part as well for the nights when the wind shifts and blows out of the Southeast. Check with your local weather station and ask for the historical wind patterns for the time frame you plan on trapping.

Another potential location to be on the lookout for is a dry culvert in the area you're trapping, as the fox will most likely be using it. Look for trails entering the culverts. Fox are curious creatures; anything unusual in the area, like a lone tree in a field or a farmer's rock pile, will be explored. Fox are shy of woods and generally like to travel about 30 feet out from the edge. But remember, what you're looking for is a funnel; a 'narrowing down spot' that will force the animal to travel through a particular area of opportunity. For example, picture two fields separated by a wooded row with a road in between. Wherever two fences intersect, the fox will hunt the edges of that intersection. Any type of sand pit is naturally attractive, as are recently cut woods with lots of deadfalls since the area will have lots of mice and rabbits. Find the food and you'll find the predator.

Now a professional fox trapper would have farms set up using this knowledge and cover about 100 miles a day in his truck. Figure 6 - 10 traps per farm, and if snaring is legal, another 6 -12 snares per farm. NOTE: Be very careful here because it is hunting season so you want to be set up on farms that don't have hunters or on preferred areas like pastures. The hunters will be working the corn and bean fields. This trapping pattern will be run for a week to ten days and then you'll rotate these traps onto new farms. You should plan on having 15 - 20 farms in each square around your house, so pick routes that take you in a square. You head East for roughly 25 miles, turn North 25 miles, turn West 25 miles and back home turning South for 25 miles. This is just an example, as you'll most likely use side roads and routes taking you all over inside of this 'square'.

Now if you repeat this in all four directions you would want 80 farms set up. This is what most new people don't understand. The trapping season may last three months, but 80 - 90% of your total catch will be caught in the first 30 days. Therefore, if you had 60 - 80 farms set up (with permission of course) you would run them for 30 days. Break this down to each direction for one week and try to stay on each farm for 7 days, then move on. You would take the cream of the crop, leaving the rest for seed for next year. But, you tell me you just want to be a part - time Mountain Man. Then get 4 - 12 farms and do the same thing; or just set up on weekends or take two weeks' vacation time. There are many options if you just think about it.

The number one set that takes 80% of the fox is the ***dirt hole set***. This is the most important set for you to master, bar none. *Everything* works the set, not just foxes. Coyotes, coon, even mink will work your sets. Learn to master this set and you will be into animals quickly.

Fishers

Fishers are a large and aggressive animal. Females run in the 6-8 pound range and males run in the 12-18 pound range. They're completely fearless about traps, and that makes them very easy to trap. I have caught them in mink pocket sets, coyote dirt holes, bobcat cubby sets, and fox dirt holes. In fact, if they are in the area you can catch them. They come to just about any kind of bait. If you're trapping them on purpose, the #220 conibear on leaning log set works great. Baited with beaver of course.

A Fisher in the Dark

For those of you not familiar with the fisher, it's in the same family as the mink. The females weigh up to 6 - 8 pounds, and the males weigh up to 12 - 15 lbs. After releasing several of these animals, I started calling them Tasmanian

Devils. I mean to tell you they're hyper, strong, and just go wild when you try to take them out of a trap. The females aren't too bad, you can cut a forked stick, hold their head down and release the trap and the animal is gone in a flash. The males, on the other hand, want to kill you from the start. I mean, I have had them pop their heads out of the forked stick and just chew their way up the stick, like corn on the cob. I let one male go and he chased me back to my truck.

I have a healthy respect for these animals, so I wised up and bought a release pole. That way, when I run my fox traps in the dark (on my way to work), I can easily release any fisher caught in my traps. So one morning, while I'm checking my traps, a large male fisher in one of them. I mean, this fellow is big, close to 20 lbs. Of course, my flashlight died when I was checking the last trap, so I could just barely see in the glow of early dawn. I placed the release noose over his neck, tightened it down and held the animal to the ground. This was working out pretty well. I stepped on the release pole and grabbed the trap lever and popped his foot out. Well, if I'd had a flashlight with me, I probably would have seen that the release noose wasn't all the way around his neck. Anyway, the strangest thing happened next. When his foot popped out of the trap, his head popped out of the noose... and the fight was on!

He grabbed a hold of my pant leg and started to climb and bite his way up my leg. Now all I can see is a dark, super-hyper animal, growling, biting, snarling its way up my leg. I kicked out as hard as I could, but the fisher had his teeth dug into my pant leg and when my leg came back, the fisher came back with it. I panicked and began kicking it in the head with my other foot and then kicked out again with the leg he was attached to. Old Taz went a-flyin'. He hit the ground at a dead run, straight back for me! If I'd had a gun, I would have shot him on the spot. But with no gun, I ran for the truck instead.

I made it back to the truck just a few steps ahead of Taz and leaped onto the hood. He circled to the other side and I quickly jumped into the truck and slammed the door. The term: 'poor defenseless animals', does not apply to fishers!!!

Raccoons

Raccoons are one of Nature's most adaptable animals. You could set a raccoon loose almost anywhere and they would survive, adapt, and even thrive in most situations. As a member of the bear clan, once fully grown they can be as fierce as a bear. A full-grown male raccoon can hold his own against a coyote twice his size. If a dog chases one into the water, they will turn on the dog, climb on his head and drown him. Raccoons semi-hibernate in winter because they have bare feet and don't like to walk on snow! But, on warm nights above 30 degrees (-1 Celsius) in snow country, you will still catch the 'big gorilla' males out looking for food. This time of year, they easily attracted to just about any kind of bait.

The life cycle of a raccoon is much like that of the fox. The males search out the den trees or other adequate den locations during the February - March time frame. The big male will mate with as many females as he can and move on. The female's job is to raise the young completely on her own. She will have anywhere from four to ten babies with six as an average. As the kits mature, they stay together as a family unit, and much like human families, once the males are large enough they may strike out on their own. Of course, nothing is written in stone; sometimes the family stays together through the following winter, sometimes they break up. The big female is your moneymaker. Finding where she is and trapping around her den can be done year after year. If you catch her too close to the den, the rest of the family will move away. It's best to trap at least ¼ mile away from the den site. Even if you take her out, one of her young female kits will most likely take over the den site.

Most people think the raccoon is a water animal because that is where their tracks are most often seen. The truth is, as a member of the bear clan the raccoon must put on large stores of fat before hibernating. In the fall trapping season they are looking for large food sources and will travel as far as necessary to find them. Cornfields are a favorite spot but also wild grapes, orchards, road-kill deer, and just about any wild fruit in season. Ranchers that supplement the feeding of their calves with corn or meal will also be prime locations for trapping raccoons. Barns with hay stacks, city dumps, farms with old stacks of cars, trucks, tractors, corn silos, abandoned farm houses, old barns – all likely locations to find raccoons. The reason people generally fail to have success when trapping raccoons is because they don't take the time to truly understand the animal. Let's look at what might happen on a 4-day fall cycle of a typical raccoon.

1st Day - The raccoon hunts the streambed catching frogs, crayfish, minnows, clams or wounded ducks. *Set some traps at the water's edge.*

2nd Day - The raccoon goes out to harvest the local cornfields and clean up the spilled corn wherever he can find it. *Set some traps in the cornfield.*

3rd Day - He's off to the closest apple tree or other fruit tree surrounded by fallen fruit. *Set your traps near the tree.*

4th Day - Today he's out to raid the feed station for the cows. You see, in a 4-day cycle, a raccoon will travel all over the place. That is why finding the den location is so important.

A den tree is normally a hollow tree. Sometimes the hollow part starts at the bottom. Look for a clean trail leading into the tree; if you look really close you can see claw marks and hair on the bark. The hollow part should go up five feet or more. A raccoon might also have a den in an old abandoned car or truck on a farm. Another good location for dens is salvage yards, but these are not as good as they used to be. With the high price of metal, the junk yards are really turning over their inventories a lot faster these days; but be sure to check these locations, just in case.

Once you find the den, stay at least ¼ mile away and figure out the four main routes leading to their different feeding areas; these are your trap locations. Raccoons are very curious animals and the old-time method of putting tin foil over the trap pan in shallow water still takes raccoons every year. The 'bone yard' on a cattle farm will be visited often, so ask the farmers if they have one. These are areas where you'll catch not only raccoons but a lot of possum as well. For every raccoon, possum, or skunk you remove, that many more ground nesting birds will survive.

The enemies of ground-nesting birds are (in order) red fox, skunk, raccoons, possums and coyotes. Once I was trapping a farm area with a bone yard on it. It was just off a hill going down into an area of thick woods. I set four traps; two dirt hole on top, one cubby set about half way down, and a dirt hole at the bottom. What did I catch?

Day 1: A monster raccoon on top.

Days 2 - 4: Three skunks in a row at the bottom and one raccoon at the middle set.

Day 5: A triple; one raccoon on top, one raccoon in the middle set and one skunk at the bottom set. There is an important lesson here if you are paying attention.

Day 6:Nothing.

Day 7:While pulling the traps I caught one last raccoon in the middle set.

Four traps over seven days brought me four raccoons and four skunks. What could I have done differently? Set more traps. The bottom set was clogged up with skunks; if I had three sets down there, I could have cleaned out the skunks quicker. Then setting fresh traps in sets 30 feet from the 'skunks caught' areas, I could have taken more raccoons by setting at least one more set in the middle, about 20 feet away from the first set. Or, if I wanted to avoid the skunks, I could have set three sets on top and three in the middle. But again, if you are eating the grouse, pheasant and ducks in the area, you would want to clean out the skunks.

I had a customer tell me about a farm he had trapped. I won't say where but it was on the outskirts of a large city. The city people were dumping their cats off in the woods when they no longer wanted them. This is the worst thing for not only the cats, but especially for the wildlife, that any person can do. The cats turn feral and are a menace to wildlife. This trapper was using #220 Conibears in a bucket set. Using six sets, the first week he trapped 27 cats. Needless to say, the farmer was jumping for joy because his wife had lost over 40 chickens to all those cats.

The next week he averaged three raccoons a day for a total of 21 raccoons in a week. Now I say average; some days he took two raccoons and other days he took four. Now before everyone freaks out about the cats - the cruelty of the city folks dumping these highly efficient predators are to blame, not the trapper. If you dump dogs and cats in the country, the farmers or rural residents will have to be the adults and remove the problem. In any decent society, a thinking, caring human being would never, ever dump an animal in the woods. If you dump these domesticated house pets in the woods, someone has to clean them out by shooting or trapping them. If left on their own, nature will take her course and they will multiply like rats. Soon not even song birds will survive in that area. As a pet owner, you are responsible for taking care of your unwanted animals by either giving them away, taking them to the Humane Society or – as a last resort - putting them down yourself. Grow up and act like a responsible adult. If you are a coward and dump your useless pets in the wilds, then don't whine and cry about when the adults clean up your mess.

Raccoons are like us; sometimes they have their mind set on a certain food and will walk away from other baits. Just like you might want steak for dinner one night and decide to drive right on by the McDonalds. If you want to take raccoons in good numbers, then learning how to snare them will really pay off. But, if you are not allowed to snare in your area, there are other ways to take raccoons in good numbers. It's just like real estate; location, location, location.

A favorite spot to trap raccoons is a beaver dam. Now not all beaver dams are equal; since beaver are the ultimate over-achievers, they will build 2-3 dams, with one of those being the main crossway dam. They may not be hunting and working a particular dam, but instead, using it to cross to get to the corn field or wherever they are heading for the night. You can't ask for a better location than a beaver dam because their world is literally narrowed down to the one-foot width of the dam. You will also pick up mink hunting the dam as well.

Now remember, if you are in the deep woods with 20 or more dams, chances are only one or two will be the main crossing for raccoons. Normally, that will be the one with the best, driest crossing. But some nights, raccoons will work all the dams. You'll want to target the one or two they are really crossing.

Trees across streams are another great location, but again, if you are on a small creek with several trees fallen across, you'll have to find the main cross-over. Trees half in and half out of the water are also a good location. Place a log set with a notch cut in the tree to hold the trap flat just under the water. This is a great set because not only raccoons but mink and muskrat use these logs as well.

Another great location is a ditch leading up to a cornfield. Pine trees are often used by raccoons, especially near roads they are crossing. Raccoons are everywhere - there are virtually no 'raccoon-free' zones. Raccoons will live deep in the swamps and close to the cornfields, and wooded to heavily populated urban areas. And don't forget the nut-laden oak, pecan, walnut and hickory trees. Remember; members of the bear clan needs lots of fat put up just before winter.

Now if you're trapping coons in good numbers, you can use the #1 - ½ coilspring if you make the following modifications: Laminate the trap jaws and replace the springs with #2 music wire base plate center swivel.

Here, close to an old building, the trails are leading away from the building toward an old abandoned farm house. Notice the different color patterns on the coons. The double on the beaver dam were mostly woodland coons, and they had a darker color overall. The hanging coon was taken in thick woods next to a cornfield and has different coloring as well. The last one was taken in open area coming out from under an old building. So pay attention to when and where you're trapping. Those differing colors can mean more money from the right buyers.

Badgers

I have never really trapped a badger on purpose. I always seem to catch them in dirt hole or flat sets intended for fox or coyotes. Badgers are ferocious fighters and a very tough, mean animal. They're strong and fierce enough to drive off a black bear. Their main diet is gophers, and they'll dig all kinds of holes in search of them. You will occasionally see them out during the day sunning themselves. If you have them in your area, make sure you are using double stakes because when a badger is caught in a trap, they can easily dig out single trap stakes. I am sure if you could find their main hole, a #220 set directly over it would take them pretty easy. However, once the snow files, they hibernate for the winter.

Skunks and Opossums

Skunks

Skunks live in ground dens and spend the winter sleeping. A large skunk den may have as many as 25 skunks sleeping in it. They raise their young in the den and emerge when the weather warms up. It is not uncommon to see skunks with large litters of 8 - 11, although 6 - 7 is more common.

Today skunk pelts sell for a an average of $10. The skunk gland sells for about $10 an ounce. If you want to take good numbers of skunk, you can usually find them in the same locations you catch foxes. Yes, you'll catch plenty of skunks in fox sets. Skunks like to stay near abandoned farm houses with lots of barns and outbuildings. If you're lucky enough to have farms like that in your area, you won't have any trouble finding skunks.

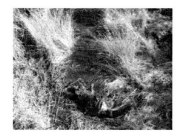

You can take them in the 110 trap using any type of stinking bait. I have caught them with fish, muskrat, beaver, and liver bait. A dirt hole set with a #1-1/2 works well.Cleaning out the skunks is very good for the homesteader, because they cause all kinds of problems. They're big-time egg eaters for one thing. They will clean out a chicken house, spray pet dogs and are the #2 worst pheasant and duck nest killer out in the wild. The #1 is the red fox. See they hunt the same area. A skunks hunting range is fairly small, about 1 - 2 miles, and they hunt that area very intensely.

They carry many different parasites and diseases, the worst of which is rabies, because of their denning habits. You must be very careful while skinning them, because they carry worms and it is not uncommon to see the worms in their flesh while you're skinning them. Wear gloves any time you are handling skunks. Their fat renders down and makes a fine gun oil. Their pelt makes a very good thick, long lasting and warm fur garment. I've heard you can eat them, but I've never had the guts to try one myself (grin). They are supposed to taste like a sweet meat.

The gland oil can be removed from the glands on either side of the anus with a hypodermic needle and stored in a bottle. A large skunk may have up to an ounce of liquid skunk oil in the two glands. It makes great fox and coyote attractor for cold weather trapping.

I once caught a skunk in a 110 conibear and I found it buried in this circle. I dug it up, took the trap off and left the skunk where it was. The next day the skunk was missing. I figure coyotes grabbed it and ran off with. They like to roll on skunks for the perfume. Anyway, I caught another skunk and decided to see what ran off with the first skunk. I buried the skunk with just the tip of the tail sticking out. Then I dug a trench leading up to the skunk. Then I buried the trap in the trench freeze-proofed it. Guess what I learned? Badgers eat skunks. He was not very happy to see me.

Opossums

The opossum is another animal that is really easy to catch. It will come into any type of bait. Opossums den under old buildings like barns and in large brushy areas. Like the coon and skunk, they hibernate for the winter. They commonly have huge litters every spring. A common sized litter is 8, and as many as 18 have been seen. During the Great Depression, many southern folks survived by eating possum. Just like coons and skunks, they are another enemy of ground nesting birds. They love raiding nests and eating the eggs. Common size ranges from 6 - 12 pounds, and I have heard of few reaching 18 pounds. The males, when cornered, can be fierce fighters. Unless they decide to play 'possum', that is.

Don't Worry, He'll Play Possum

When I was a teenager, my younger brother and I were walking home one night. We cut through an open field and ran across a possum. Not by any means a large possum, only a little 5 or 6 pounder.

It was a cool fall night, and the prime pelt was worth some money. Since we were in an open field, I had to run back to the wood line for a stick to properly dispatch the animal with. As I ran off, I told my younger brother to go up and kick it and it will play possum. Playing possum, is when the animal feels it is in mortal danger and it will play dead. The animal actually slows its heart beat down and appears not to be breathing.

My younger brother was always impressed by my vast outdoor knowledge. He ran up to it believing what I said was true and kicked the possum. The theory must be true you know, the old timers have told me my whole life. Well, guess what the possum didn't do? How did you guess ?

My brother kicked him a good one and the possum took a roll and came up fighting. No, the possum is not known for his fierce fighting skills. But, I'm here to tell you he is no slouch either. So I grabbed a stick and came running back, just in time to see my brother running toward me. Right behind him is this little possum, all teeth and coming up quick. I dispatched the animal with one blow to the head. Adrenaline is amazing stuff. And you know, for some reason to this day, 20 some odd years later, my brother still talks about not listening to me for some reason.

When I was teenager, possums were selling for around $3-$8 dollars each. Now remember, gas was about $.50 a gallon and a dozen #1-1/2 coil spring traps cost $29.95. It wasn't uncommon to get $5 a night average trapping possums. At the first snow, the possum would head for their winter dens. It was simple to track them down and put a #220 over the den hole.

The best set for possums is a dirt hole like you make for fox. A perfectly made up set will almost guarantee that a possum will beat the fox to it and ruin the set by getting caught. Don't worry about over trapping them. You can wipe them out on a farm and in a few years they will be back just as thick as before.

Weasels sets

The weasel, also known as ermine, turns from brown to white in the winter. The weasel is fearless, and will readily enter bare, uncovered traps in search of food. A favorite set of mine uses the old style #1 underspring. These days, you have to buy these traps used, if you can find them at all.

Using a 3 pound coffee can with lid, cut a small hole in the lid and set the trap inside. Punch a few holes in the bottom of the can in order to allow the scent to flow from the back of the can

and out the front. That way they will approach from the front and go right to work getting themselves caught in the trap.

The trap should be baited with a bloody meat, such as muskrat, beaver or liver. Another successful catch!

If you can't find a #1 underspring, you can still use the can without the lid, leaving the long spring sticking out of the can. Note the tracks in the snow coming up to the can. Another nice weasel in the trap! The set having been re-made, you can see the long spring

sticking out in front of the can. This set will also take mink so make sure you wire the trap off to something solid.

Squirrels

There are five different squirrels considered as food. The fox, gray, black, red and the ground squirrel. Squirrels, like rabbits, have many enemies including: hawks, owls, foxes, coyotes, and if you have them in your area, marten and fisher.

If you have ever watched a squirrel in the woods, you will have noticed that they are a nervous and hyperactive animal, quick to raise the alarm.

If you have squirrels in your area, they are easy to trap or snare. They are one of the few animals where I recommend using homemade snares, depending on their size. To get into squirrels quickly, use 22 gauge galvanized wire made into a small loop of 2 ½" to 3". Place the loop ½" above a tree branch on a known run and you won't have long to wait. You can also set up a long pole between feed trees to trap them on. Because of all their enemies, squirrels like to stay off the ground. Set these up in the summer and allow the squirrels to get use to using them for the fall trapping season.

A #110 conibear with a rag tied to the trigger with a little peanut butter on it works like a champ. I helped one customer out who was out of work and need to get through the winter. He took 27 squirrels in 2 weeks with four #110 conibears. It is easy to overharvest squirrels, so don't trap the same spot for more than two weeks unless you are in a real hot spot.

Squirrels are very good eating and the fox squirrels have a very tough hide for tanning and making into long lasting work gloves. The red squirrels live in the pine forest and survive on pine nuts. They are the little ones you always see while deer hunting. They yell at you and tell the whole world where you're sitting. I always thought of buying a pellet pistol for shooting them to keep them quiet but never tried it.

With ground squirrels, there are certain areas where you should never trap them. In Wyoming, Montana and parts of North Dakota, the prairie dogs and ground squirrels may be infected with bubonic plague. I know of a fellow who helped a friend in Wyoming skin a bobcat, and he died the next day. You just never know...The bobcat had been eating prairie dogs that carried bubonic plague. All it took is a small nick in the skin on his hand. The blood from the plague-infected bobcat then entered his bloodstream and he died shortly thereafter. After reading that story, I bought skinning gloves and use them most of the time now, depending on what I am skinning. I didn't tell you that to scare you away from trapping and skinning wild game. You just need to take the proper precautions in order to stay healthy. It is always best to check with your state Fish and Wildlife people and ask them about possible disease in animals in your area and what signs and symptoms to look for. Many of our earlier ancestors survived eating squirrels and I have eaten hundreds with nary a problem.

The #220 Conibear

The #220 conibear is a wonderful trap. I have talked to several beginner's who, after catching 10 - 12 coons in a week their first year, asked me "why do I even have to use leg-holds?". I'll answer that question later on in the book. Like I said before, if you had 4 - #220 conibears you would be able to catch plenty of coons to eat, especially if you're in a state with a large coon population like Iowa or Nebraska. Most of the southern states also have large coon populations, and most of the northern states have good coon numbers. There are coons out west too, but not the high numbers you see elsewhere.

I'll say it again: You, as a trapper, have to be responsible. The #220 conibear will kill dogs and cats, so make sure you're off the beaten trail before you make any sets. Here in Michigan, we have to have the #220 in dog-proof boxes or four feet off the ground. If you're trapping a farm, explain to the farmer that you plan on using #220's on the ground and if it's ok with him, then ask where to set the traps so no dog or cat gets caught. I trap farms that want every coon gone and the farmer is responsible. They tie their pets up, and I don't set any #220's within 1/4 of a mile from a road or building.

There was a case last fall in New York that upset a bunch of people. A new trapper was setting dry 12" culverts at the _edge of the road!_. Someone was taking their dog for a walk and the dog stuck his head in the trap and was killed. The owner raised hell, and had a right to, because that's irresponsible on the trapper's part and no one wants to lose a loved pet. Please make sure you follow the 1/4 mile rule. I try my best to avoid catching pets. Enough on that. Just remember there is no second chance for most pets with the conibear #220, unless it's a big dog. Then, maybe…

Setting the #220

Note the Setting tool is painted orange to make it easier to keep track of in the field.

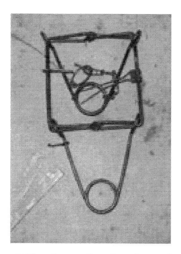

Open one spring and flip the safety latch to the outside as shown.

To set the #220, use the setting tool to compress the springs. Simply hook the tool into the eye of the spring and squeeze. Hold the tool with one hand, and with the other flip the safety catch on. Do the same to the other spring. The trap is not set yet, so place the trap on the ground and spread it open to hold the springs in place. Flip the two prong triggers out of the square, place your knee on the other end and push down. (This will open the trap.)

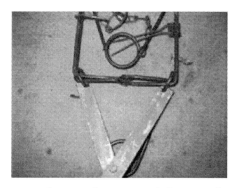

Hook the setting tool into the eyes of the conibear springs and squeeze until you are able to flip the safety latch on the spring. Hold the spring tightly while doing that.

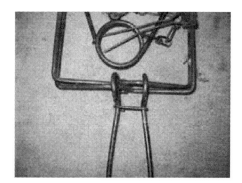

The safety latch is now in place. Now repeat the procedure on the second spring

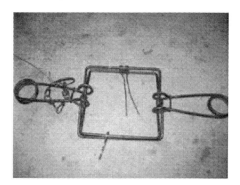

Note the springs are centered. This square jaw design was last made in the 70's. That just shows that well taken care of traps can last for 30 or more years.

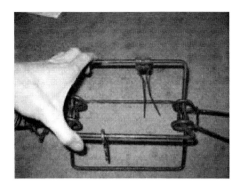

Note pull the jaws together using both hands. Make sure once you get them together you slide the safety latch down on the spring so it stays tight. Not responsible for personnel; injury do so at you own risk.

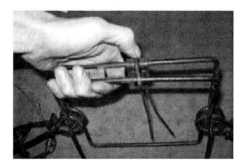

Note: be careful to keep pressure on the jaws until you feel that the trap is held by the trigger. Keep pressure on the top with your thumb and SLOWLY remove your finger from inside the jaws of the trap.

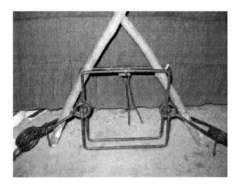

The #160, #220#, #280 and #330 all set this way. When setting in the woods, you want 2 sticks as shown, angled in the jaws of

the trap. This prevents the animal from knocking the trap over. The sticks are shoved into the ground to hold the trap firmly in place. Don't forget to remove the safety latches. Be careful, these traps have never broken any of my fingers, but they do smart like getting hit with a hammer. Remember, in freezing conditions you want to place sticks under the bottom jaws to keep the trap off the ground. Otherwise the sun can heat the steel up and cause it to melt in the ground then freeze when the sun goes down. Just small 3-4 inch long sticks about 1-2 inch diameter will work.

Next, make sure the safety latches are still in place and slide them back toward the spring end. Then grab both sides of the trap, holding it set. Set just like the #110; flip the slotted part of the trigger to the slot in between the two prongs, Now the trap is set. If you're setting in a 5-gallon bucket to make it almost dog proof, this is how you do it. Small beagle size dogs can get into the bucket so you still have to be very careful where you make your set. Cut the plastic bucket with two 7-inch slots on each side - one for each spring. The trap will slide back into the two slots. The slots only have to be just a bit wider than the springs. Then cut a 6 inch round hole in the lid. Place the trap inside, leaving the safety latches on and pop the lid on and you have a dog-proof box.

Place the bucket between two logs so it won't roll. Wire off to a small tree and you're ready to bait and set. First, place bait in the bucket, a dab of lure on the bait, trap, lid and sticks, and to insure the bucket won't move back place against a tree. Last thing, after everything else is done, take the safety latches off and you've got a bucket set. When you make up the buckets, test them with a long stick to insure the trap closes tight with the lid on. A friend of mine uses this set-up in barns with great results. He keeps changing the bait with the buckets until every coon is caught. The farmer loves him for it, but new coons move in every year and it's an ongoing battle. He had one coon that wouldn't come in for fish, lure or corn. So one morning he was cooking bacon and saved the grease. He added two drops of peppermint to the grease, along with some peanut butter and tried it out. The coon was caught the next morning.

#220 Bucket Set for Raccoons

Set the #220 on top of the bucket with the springs folded out and mark the top of the bucket, as in the picture, on both sides.

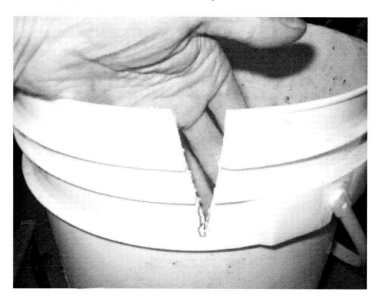

Next, cut a 'V' notch in each side of the bucket where you marked it earlier.

Now set the #220 so it's ready to fire. Place it in the V's you cut earlier as illustrated. See how the #220 fits perfectly? Bait the bucket in the back and this setup will work for fishers or coons. Green buckets blend in a little better in the woods but the coons don't mind white.

Now set it on the ground. In the woods, you want the back of the bucket against a tree with rocks or firewood chunks on the sides so it can't roll. Add bait and lure in the back in you're in

business. Obviously, you add the bait and lure first, then set the trap.

Warning: This set, when on the ground will take dogs and cats and may be illegal in some states. To prevent catching dogs, set on a leaning pole 6-10 inches in diameter and nail or wire the bucket to the pole 4 feet off the ground with the pole at a 45 degree angle.

It's best to set these up before trapping season and pre-bait them so it teaches the coons to use them. Then once trapping season comes, add the trap.

Setting Traps on Animal Trails

All animals have trails. When you find a small trail going through thick brush, you'll find a spot all narrowed down with brush over the top. This is a perfect place for a trail set. On the farm I trap, I walk along the edge of the woods looking for coon trails. The coons drag the corn into the woods so the trail is easy to find. Just follow the trail, and if you can't find a narrow spot, make one with sticks and wire. If you're in a high coon area, you can set 1 to 4 traps on one trail. If you only have four #220's, then find all the trails before the season starts and narrow down 4 spots on each trail. There can be up to ten trails coming into a 40-acre field. Set the traps, check them and move to the next trail every day. You can trap the cream of the crop from all the different coon families feeding in the field. In a top area you could get 2 coons a night for 10 nights for a total of 20 coons. The average price for coon fur is $8.00 down south and up to an $18.00 average on top grade northern coon. (Prices on fur vary every year and I'm quoting 1997's prices as an example) But even at $8.00 each, 20 coons is $160. That's not a bad way to help pay for your equipment costs. And besides, look at all the coon meat you get to eat. Coon is good eating, but that's another story.

If I was trapping with only four #220's this is how I'd set up: I'd put two on the trail along with two bucket sets. The best almost guaranteed set up is done by conditioning the coons. Two weeks before trapping season opens, set out 10 buckets without the traps, but baited with fish heads. The idea is to get the coons used to climbing into the bucket to get a free meal. Bait them once a week. Then when the season opens set your four traps.

The next day, when you move the traps, move the four to the next trail with the already baited buckets. Then take the 2 buckets and move to a new trail and pre-bait, get it? Just keep rotating. If you're lucky enough to find a farm with a pond then you can trap the muskrats in the pond at the same time. One farm with 4 coon traps, 6 muskrats traps and, if you're real lucky, a couple of beaver will be there so you can set your #330's, then you'll have all your traps set out. If one farm doesn't have all this, then trap on two farms. That's all there is to it.

Get permission, of course, before trapping on farms. Talk to the farmer, and trap only where he wants you to. I carry a 22 rifle with me and add grouse and rabbits as I'm checking traps. Take the kids along. They love trapping and hunting and being with Dad. I have a trapping buddy who has taken all of his kids from the time they were 5 years old. His 10-year-old caught his first mink last year. Every year I take a friend and his son along the trapline with me. The kid has more fun than both of us, and his Dad doesn't even trap.

The younger you start the kids, the better the chance they'll have to learn to accept the cycles of life in the wilds. If you leave it up to public education, the teachers and Disney will fill their heads with Bambi and Thumper and misconceptions of cruelty to animals. It will be better for the children to learn this lesson now before a survival situation occurs where they might refuse to eat the meat or wear the fur. They need to understand that their health and maybe their very survival could depend on their acceptance of these basics.

Trapping Groundhogs

If a farmer has groundhog problems, you can sometimes make a deal with him. Offer to trap the groundhogs for him now, in return for permission to trap for fur during the season. Groundhogs are easy to trap. As a friend of mine used to say, "I wasn't sure what was using the hole, so a #220 solved that mystery."

Place the #220 over the groundhog hole at the angle of the hole. Stabilize the trap and take the safety off. Don't forget to wire it off. If there is nothing to wire off to, then use a stake or a sharpened stick pounded in to the ground. Show the farmer the dead ones, then skin them and sell the hides to fishermen who use the fur for tying flies.

Another set for the #220 is the cubby set, which works well for bobcats. I like making these next to beaver dams because the bobcat likes to hunt around the dams. All you do is make a small box against a tree (remember the wind) out of sticks. Cover the top with pine boughs and stabilize the #220 with sticks. Now, I'll tell you how to get the bobcats. Use a beaver head and tail for bait and use my beaver lure. The bobcat love to eat beaver and beaver lure makes it smell like a fresh kill, so the bobcat goes in for a free meal and gets a free neck brace instead. Works like a champ.

There's one last thing. Make sure if you're using bait or lure that you're set up for the wind. The animal has to smell it in order to get caught. So the wind should come across the back of the bucket toward the trail. I will talk wind, location and good equipment over and over again. Pay attention to wind so you can get paid for all your hard work.

Chapter 5: Water Trapping

Canoe Scouting and Lessons Learned

I recently floated a river scouting for fur sign. My cousin Larry was with me and we learned a lot together about nature, animals, camping and fishing. There's nothing better in the world than being out with someone  who appreciates the great outdoors and is always ready to learn something new. We always try different things to make the trip more comfortable and enjoyable for both of us.

 The first lesson I observed was on muskrat sign. I was looking for fresh muskrat droppings on a log submerged halfway into the water. I wanted one with lots of sign positioned in the sun so I could get a clear picture of it. The first thing I noticed was the currents effect on the muskrat sign. Muskrats will usually avoid the faster current, even if there is good food there. I decided that the muskrats didn't want to fight the current because it just wasn't worth the energy to obtain the food. The next thing I noticed was the logs the muskrat chose to leave droppings on. Some were out in the open, but had only a few droppings. The muskrats seemed to prefer logs that had been washed down into the middle of the river with part of them underwater. The muskrats seemed to like floating in-between this dip and would feed and rest on either side of the log. Where do you think the best sign was?

After 2 days of floating, I learned that muskrats prefer lots of overhead cover. That is where I usually saw the best sign. They liked slow moving current, with grass and roots overhanging in the water. The best log was a small 3-inch diameter log paralleling the shoreline with a nice tall pine tree directly above it. The muskrats on this little log had several piles of droppings, as many as 15, from a few old to many fresh ones.

I reasoned then that the area had a high owl population and the muskrat soon learned to feed under cover before the silent death from above swooped down and ruined the night. Once you get in the habit of thinking like a muskrat and knowing where to look for sign, you will quickly discover more sign.

The next lesson on fur that I observed concerned the river beaver. They preferred to set up bank dens and they range as far as 1/2 mile up and down from the den. Rarely were many dens close together. But I think that was due more to available food supply than anything else. And I found that the beaver also prefer the slower current. Sometimes I would find their den in the slow current just before rapids. I would swing the canoe down beside any log that was parallel the river and was stuck out from the shore by 1 - 2 feet. By looking carefully, I could make out the trail of the beaver swimming beside the log and his back feet would scrape the bottom. This is a good set for a #330 conibear. I also observed several trails that showed where the beavers climbed up on the bank of the river in search of food. Every side drainage, creek or run off with water in it had fur sign. Those are a definite fur magnet. Every one with water in it had beaver, muskrat, coon, and sometimes even mink sign.

As I walked along the drainage area, sometimes I would see a beaver dam. Beyond that first dam, there was always a coon trail. Sometimes a bobcat trail could be made out as well. I think the animals that hunt the area soon learn where the beaver dams are, and especially the coon and mink learn to hunt the dams for fish, crawfish, and frogs.

Further fur sign in the area that I observed was evidenced by logs lying across the river. Some logs had a clear trail leading up to them. If you look closely at the log, you can make out faint claw marks from different animals using this as a bridge.

The river is always a source of fur and there are many lessons to be learned if you will just take the time to look and see what's there. The fur is there, it is your job to not only find the sign, but also to figure it out.

Now where should you trap? Always set the small waterways that flow into the main river. Look for cover that will protect the muskrat and for natural crossings over the river to take advantage of easy sets. The signs are easy to see if you just look for them. Try to think like the animal you want to trap. Think of predators and of the easiest way for them to hunt and cross. Then the picture will become clear in your mind.

The next lesson was from a new water filter I purchased. The water filter fits into a canteen, and you fill the canteen up with river water. After filling the canteen, screw the filter and cap on and squeeze out the filtered water. This is incredible, after seeing how well this works. I bought two, but the first one was junk. I bought it the year before from a popular surplus place. It took two hands squeezing (like you're Arnold Schwarzeneger) for 5 minutes to get one cup of water. This new one is awesome, it squeezed easy and the water is well filtered. It will filter up to 200 gallons of water. What is great about this is it frees you up from carrying the added weight of extra water. Plus, when the canteen became warm from the summer heat, I would just dump the water out, find a cool clean spot in the river and refill it. There's nothing like having cool, fresh, clean water during the heat of the day.

The next lesson was on bears. When dealing with bears, I do some things by habit that you may not be aware of. First, when you are in bear country, you should always keep a clean camp. After eating your meal, be sure to clean up after yourself. Wash the dishes and burn the cans so there is no smell left on them. If you have fish, clean them in the river and make sure you throw everything in the water. Then mark your territory. I know this sounds funny, but it has always worked for me. When the call of nature comes, have everyone go around different sides of the camp and mark the area. It really works.

Do all four sides and if you are going to be there any length of time, make sure you do this the whole time you are in that campsite. Bears are still afraid of humans, so if a bear approaches the camp from the downwind, he will get wind of one of the spots and leave. Of course, this is a general rule that has always worked for me. However, there is nothing like having a 12 gauge shotgun with slugs to help you sleep better at night.

Now, since I was talking about camping, I'd like to share my bannock recipe with you. My cousin had it made by someone else before the trip and it didn't really work out that well. That turned out to be a chewy, half cooked dough, that was not very good. I don't like carrying bread when I'm in the bush because it is always getting smashed to pieces. So, I read up on how the old trappers used to scout for weeks at a time and made their own bread. The recipe is quite simple. All you need is flour, baking soda, salt, water, and butter or some type of oil for the pan.

You build your fire and as it is burning down to coals you mix 3/4 cup of flour, one tablespoon of baking powder, a little salt and then mix the dry ingredients together. Slowly add water and mix into a dough that is stiff. Don't add too much water. You want it like bread dough, not like a thin pancake mix . I have an enamel 7-inch frying pan that is perfect for this. Place the pan on the coals of the fire to heat up. Add butter and wait until it is melted and the pan is lightly coated. Add your dough and spread it out into the size of a pita loaf. Cook one side until you can flip it over without it breaking in half. This is best done on a medium heat away from the flame. Once flipped, add some more butter and cook. The bread will rise about 1/2 to 3/4 of its wet size. Check for doneness by sticking it with a sliver of wood until no dough sticks to it.

This is really awesome bread. Its like having fresh bread baked every time. We made peanut butter and jam sandwiches by cutting the loaf in half. Try it with summer sausage, eat it with baked beans, cook it for breakfast to go with the eggs. We cooked up 4 pieces of bacon, 3 eggs, and one loaf each for breakfast. That breakfast gave us plenty of energy for 5 hours of paddling on the river, hauling the canoe over logs, and walking up small streams. I was even surprised at how long I was full and had energy.

We fished and had some pretty fair luck. I did find that the trout preferred the Panther Martian spinner, about 8 to 1 over Mepps spinners. The river had brown trout and they were fairly fussy. I averaged about two strikes per hole and then that hole was done. If the fish could see you, they would not strike.

Next trip I will re-float the same river and will take a notebook. I'll do that in order to figure out how many traps and what kind I will need for this stretch of river. I will also set up little sticks and logs in the trails so the animals will get used to walking or swimming through certain narrowed down spots. Until next time, have fun and remember you are always learning.

A Canoe trapping story

The canoe drifted silently down the river. I was a lone traveler reliving the ancient culture of harvesting fur from the wild. I gazed silently in amazement at the beauty of nature. The deep blackness of the water was a stark contrast against the bright sky overhead. This is always a sign that winter is closing in. The trees have lost their foliage and the animals are in panic mode, frantically trying to either put on fat or store enough food for the winter.

I believe that only a trapper sees the wilderness as it really is, for he knows what travels this land. A wet log with a stray scratch on it has a meaning. Fresh cattail cuttings piled on a feed bed has a meaning. A pile of mud with a unique musky smell has a meaning. The tiny trail leading to the hollow log has a meaning, and the smoothness of a fallen log across the river has a meaning. Many different animals call this home. Do you know all the ones I'm talking about? I will check the tracks in the snow walking on top of the beaver hut every time I come through this area because I'm a trapper. And as a trapper, I know that deep in the wilderness, far from civilization, lies the beauty and peacefulness of nature. Understanding the complexity of nature will require a lifetime of study.

As I round a curve in the river, a flock of mallards breaks off the water and fly through the gray haze over the water. Since I'm not duck hunting, I sit back and enjoy the show just for the pleasure of it. The greenheads race to gain altitude, their glossy whispering in the still air, and soon they have vanished from sight. As I approach the next trap, the excitement builds as I wonder if luck will be on my side today. The trap is empty and it doesn't appear that any animal has approached this set. So I steer the canoe back out in the current and move on to the next. The silence is pierced by something banging on a log. The huge pleated head woodpecker is startled by my appearance and flies off to find another tree. He is one of the largest of the woodpecker clan. An animal breaks the surface in front of the canoe and then disappears with a plunge back into the water. Was that a muskrat or a mink? As I drift down toward a deep hole, I see a trout jump out of the water and skip across the surface like a flat stone. I can see the wild panic in the trouts eyes, as right behind him, an animal surfaces in hot pursuit. I instantly recognize the animal as an otter. In the next instant, another otter surfaces farther downstream with the trout in his mouth. What an awesome rare glimpse into the world of the otter.

Otters travel in a huge hunting circle, so they may not be in this area again for a month or more. The otter closest to me made a warning call when he saw the canoe, and they both disappeared immediately under water. I continue down the river where the next trap is coming; up a hollow log set. The trap, a #1-1/2 coilspring, is baited with fish and carefully buried in front of the log. I see a movement and the excitement builds. What is it? As I get closer, a high pitch scream shattered the silence! Then I see that it's a beautiful silky black mink, held firmly in my trap. The mink screams in an effort to scare off larger predators. A quick tap on the head with a stick knock him out. Then I place a #110 conibear on his neck, remove him from the #1-1/2 coilspring trap and put him in the water. The combination of the conibear and water should kill him quickly. I carefully remake the set, delighted because it is all set up with fresh mink urine now. Once the set is remade, I put the mink in the canoe and the journey continues. What a wonderful life. What a privilege and honor it is to see sights that only a trapper can see.

As I round another bend, I approach a log set for muskrats. This is one of those sets you dream about finding. A fallen log with a dip under water about 8" wide. Muskrat droppings are on both sides of the log. A #1 long spring is set up in the middle. Now this is where experience pays off. The dog of the trap is facing shore. Why is this important to know? Because, if the muskrat climbs up on the log from the water side and set the trap off with his foot on the dog, it will actually push his foot out of the trap as it fires. Now you have a trap shy muskrat. But, with the dog on the shore side, the trap closes on the foot. Once the muskrat realizes he's been caught, he dives into deep water and quickly drowns.

Three feet of 14 gauge wire is attached to the trap and to a stake out in deep water. There is also another three foot stake off to one side, about 12 inches away from the first stake. You drive this second stake in so that 6" remains above water. The muskrat will swim in a circle and get tangled up on this stake and drown. That's why it is commonly referred to as a tangle stake. Well, the trap is missing, and that means another catch. I swing the canoe over to shore and bank it, then want walk out to the set. Wrapped around the tangle stake is a thoroughly caught muskrat. I pull the stake up and unwrap the wire, then I remove the muskrat from the trap and put it on the log. I then replace the tangle stake and re set the trap. A little trick I use is to find a large water soaked maple leaf and carefully place it inside the trap jaws. This breaks up the outline of the trap and makes the muskrat think it is a safe place to put his foot down.

After I get the canoe back in the water, I take a moment to reflect on my good fortune. I realize that I have never felt more alive than when running a canoe trapline. You learn the feel of the land and you can sense a weather change coming. It's at times like this that you will truly see nature and appreciate her majesty. At noon I stop in my lunch area for a bite to eat. Before the season opened, I had built a lean-to constructed of 6 inches of pine boughs, with a reflector wall positioned so the heat from the fire reflects back into the lean-to. A handy stump takes the place of a chair. I cook up lunch and make a fresh pot of coffee. A can of Campbell soup with cold sandwiches brightens the day. Before leaving camp, I top off the thermos with coffee and head downstream.

The next trap is a sight to see. A raccoon is caught in a mink pocket set. The way the trap was set up, there was a 2 inch branch above the set. The raccoon had pulled the branch down and climbed on top of it. He must have fallen off a couple of times because the trap chain was wrapped around the branch. That was a lucky break for me, because the springing of the branch had pumped the trap stake out of the ground. The raccoon was free to run away if he had only figured out how to unwrap the trap chain off the branch. I popped the coon with my .22 and put him in the canoe. I reset the trap, but cut the branch out of the way just in case. I might not be so lucky next time.

As I drift silently down stream, I spot a doe standing beside the stream looking downstream and away from me. I drifted the canoe closer until I got within a few feet of her. I love watching the reaction when they finally see me. As the canoe passed into her field of view, she whipped her head around and quick as a blink, she was 20 feet away! She was standing there looking at me with her eyes bugging out, wondering if I am for real. This is a good stream for picking up muskrats, mink, beaver and raccoons. The next set along the way is a mud pile set. The beaver had been feeding in this area, so I set a #4 double-longspring, knowing that would do the job.

One of the tricks to catching beaver is to use a poke stick along with a trap bed dug on the shoreline. The beaver will normally move forward until their chest hits the shore and then step out of the water. If you just set the trap under 1 inch of water, the beavers chest will set it off, and you will have a trap shy beaver to deal with. Do it right the first time.

As I approach the set, I see a beaver tail floating next to the deep water stake. With this setup, a stake is pounded in on shore and wire is fed through a swivel that only allows the trap to go to move in one direction, toward deep water. Otherwise the beaver can get back shore and won't drown. I pull the beaver out and remake the set. This is a medium sized beaver weighing around 35 pounds. That will make for some good eating, I guarantee.

I set off again and head toward a bank den set that's next in line. The set is a #110 conibear I've set for muskrat. One more muskrat added to the catch. I see a grouse walking on a log, and before he stops and looks around, I whip my .22 up and fire. More meat for the pot. Grouse are one of the best tasting wild game birds, in my opinion. I add him to the growing pile in the canoe. Before long, I realize the light is starting to fade as the landing comes into view. It has been another wonderful and successful day on the trapline. I land the canoe and haul all of my catch and equipment to the truck, then haul the canoe up for the day. But my trapping day isn't over yet. When I get home, I still have to skin the animals, flesh the pelts and put them on stretchers. Then I have to get the meat processed and wrapped for the freezer.

It's a wonderful life, floating a section of river like that for seven days. And that's all it should take to clean up the surplus animals. Now I'll pull the traps and rotate into a new area next week. If I could do only one type of trapping, it would be canoe trapping.

Mink

Think of mink as coming from the same family as the weasel. You have the short-tailed weasel, the long-tailed weasel, mink, marten, fisher and wolverines. The mink is an awesome hunter that spends most of its life killing anything it can get its teeth on including ducks, muskrats, frogs, trout, crayfish, clams,

minnows, mice, voles, and just about anything else it can catch. They are hyper little animals ranging in size from 1 - 2 pounds for the males and 1/2 to 1-1/2 pounds for the females. They're prolific travelers and cover a long distance that normally ranges in a week to 10 day circle. Being the hyper killer they are, they like to hunt and hunt until making a large kill then find a small burrow to curl up and sleep. They mostly hunt at night but it's not uncommon to see them during the day. The male mates and then splits the scene. The female raises the young and drives them off in the fall.

Mink are incredibly fast; I once watched a mink attack baby ducks and faster than I could see four of the babies were killed amid squawking and duck feathers flying and water splashing. In fact, it happened so quick that I didn't know what was killing the ducks until the rest escaped and the mink grabbed one of the dead ones and swam a short distance away to eat it. Mink tend to go into a killing frenzy in a chicken house with the feathers flying and blood spewing and the chickens squawking in panic. That mink will keep killing chickens until there are none left to kill. In fact, the farmer I bought my house from told me about the 40 chickens he was raising for fryers. A mink came in and killed 36 in one night.

Trapping mink is normally done with a #1-1/2 coil spring, the #11 double long spring or the #110 or #120 conibear. Mink will come to bait, but they prefer fresh bait. Some trappers salt their fish to keep them fresh. To take mink in high numbers you need to cover a huge area, running 200 traps or more, covering 100 miles of trapline a day or more.

Most mink are taken with a pocket set, which is a different type of dirt hole set normally set next to the edge of stream or river. A hole is dug straight back into a bank about 10 - 12 inches deep and baited in the back with a #1-1/2 placed right in front of the hole. Now the important thing to remember about mink traps is to have them adjusted to fire on 4 ounces of weight. That's why a lot of trappers like the #11 trap, because it's easy to adjust and has the power to hold a coon. Trust me, you are going to trap a lot of coons in your mink sets.

Mink spend a lot of time in the water, so you will occasionally take them in your muskrat set trying to enter muskrat dens. A favorite set is near bridges on the downstream side where there is normally a deep hole that narrows down. On the narrowed down part, right on the edge of the bank, set a #110 on both sides under water. The #110 is placed with the spring facing deep water. If you have to, cut the bank with your trowel so you have the trap jaws right up against the bank. Now this doesn't work well early in the season, because the mink are still hunting the shore line. But, when the weather changes and ice starts to form, it becomes a great location for this type of set. If you just want mink, then like everything else you want a variety of traps set out; #110 in the water, pocket sets, and homemade cubby sets. Cubbies can be made out of wood just large enough to hold a #110 conibear in the front. These are made in the summer and left out in your trapping area to age in the weather. You can even place hay on the bottom to encourage the mice to start using them. The mink will hunt the mice and get used to going inside looking for the mice they smell. You can make them out of plastic or steel pipe. You can also snare mink using the small game snare using tiny loops 3 inches in diameter. You have to find the tiny trails in the weeds but if you look closely, you'll find them.

People get frustrated trapping mink because they don't understand the animal. The mink travels great distances, and if you're only trapping for one week you might not get a chance at one. I remember one year I set up under this little bridge with a small stream, where I set a #110 conibear right against the wall. I used a rock to hold the trap in place. It took me three weeks to catch the mink. Why so long? The mink is busy travelling and it's hard to predict when he'll come by your set. Mink trapping requires a large dose of patience.

Now, it's possible to catch mink the first time you check your sets too. It all depends on how many mink are in the area, and how you're trapping, numbers of traps etc… I can't say for sure whether any animal is smart or dumb, but I do know that some have been educated by careless trappers. All it takes is one bad experience with a trap set and the animal learns. And each animal will handle the bad experiences differently. Lots of mink trappers work the bridges. So mink learn to get out of the water and run up the hill, cross the road and come down past the bridge before they start hunting again. Others will swing out and swim down the middle, avoiding the edges. Others may change their travel pattern to avoid the bridge entirely. It doesn't mean these mink are un-trappable. It just means that the normal pocket set or edge set on the edge of the bridge won't take these mink. A pocket set takes most mink. It is very good set to learn to trap raccoons also.

For mink you want good cover, a brushy area with a bank next to a stream.

Using your trapping trowel, dig a hole straight back into the bank about 12 inches deep. Dig a trench so the water flows into the trench and hole. The hole is dug at a slight angle upward so the bait isn't sitting in the water. This is early season set used before freeze up.

A #1 1/2 coil spring is used. Note the trench is just big enough for the trap. The trap is cocked to one side and placed under water. Wiggle the trap into the mud to bed. But remember, not too deep.

Use a large chunk of fish for bait. Note the small stick. This is to be placed in the back of the hole, stuck into the dirt to hold the bait just off the water. It's important to make sure at least part of the bait is above water. This will make a better scent trail coming out of the hole.

Here is a picture of the mink pocket set fully complete and ready for the next mink to come along.

Mink Tunnel Set

This is a simple, yet very effective set. The bait is placed in the middle, with a #110 conibear on both ends.

In the spring or summer, go to the junk yard and find some 8 inch thin wall stovepipe. Saw off a 30 inch length for this project. Note: This will only work for 110 conibears. Cut a tapered notch on each end, about 8 inches long. The reason for the notches being so deep is that mink pretty smart animals, and you want the conibears recessed inside the ends of the pipe. The springs will slide into these notches. So the mink will travel that first 8 inches and feel comfortable and confident. With this setup, the trap is inside the pipe and well protected from the weather. It will keep the snow and freezing rain off of the conibears and the trap will keep right on working for you. Once you've got your pipes cut to length and the notches cut, you should place them out in your trapping area near small streams rivers and ponds. Cover them with hay or straw and toss some inside as well. This will cause the mice to start using them and the mink will start hunting the mice.

Here's a better look at that notch. When you slide the set #110 into the notch, the spring will lock in place and the trap will be solid. It can't be knocked over by the mink.

And here you can see the #110 in place, ready for action.

The bait in this case is a large chunk of fish. Put the bait in the center of the pipe before adding the last #110. Put your lure right on the chunk of fish.

Here, you see the completed set. What you can't see in the picture is that both #110's are wired off to the same stake. Make the tunnel blend in with its surroundings by covering it with hay, straw and leaves. Your goal is to make it look as natural as possible.

Here's a long tail weasel I caught in the tunnel set. He made it past the first conibear and ate on the muskrat, then ran into the other conibear. He is mixed pelt which means he has not turned all the way white but what a beautiful pelt for the wall. The fur buyers don't like these ones to buy because they want the pure white but these are great to home tan and sell yourself.

Muskrat Trapping

Muskrats are one of the easier animals to trap, and once you learn the secrets to trapping them you can quickly catch a pile of them. First, you need to understand the animal you are trapping. In the fall, muskrats will

build huts using cattails or other water plants and mud. Here is a picture of one. They're not difficult to recognize once you know what they are and why they're there.

 Trapping the den, or hut, is simple. All you need is hip boots, a #110 conibear, some trap wire and a suitable stick. First, find the den entrance, which is where you'll set the conibear. To find the entrance, look the den over carefully, and normally, you'll find the entrance on the deepest side. Approach the den slowly, being careful not to muddy the water. If the water is clear, sometimes you can see the run. The run is a trench normally 4 - 6 inches deeper than the surrounding bottom. If you can't see it, no big deal. Just slowly walk around the den and you will feel the trench. Using you foot, follow it into the den entrance. The entrance to the den is normally a round 5 - 6 inch hole about 10 - 12 inches deep. In real cold weather areas, they may be up to 30 inches deep. Set the #110 and wire it to the stick.

After the trap is set, run the stick through the spring at a 45 degree angle into the top corner of the square part of the conibear. This keeps the trap from getting knocked over. This is very hard to show in pictures, but hopefully you can see what I'm trying to explain here.

 It is quite common to have success on the first night when trapping muskrats. Note all the seaweed on the trap. That makes the trap blend right in. Remove the muskrat and reset the trap. Once you get a handle on this type of trapping, it is super easy to clean out muskrats in a hurry.

Another good location to set up is near an active feed bed. When you see fresh cattail cuttings like this, you know there is activity in the area and you can generally be assured of success.

Here you see the results from one night of trapping, using ten #110 conibears. I was trying for 10 for 10, but only managed to take 7 muskrats from 10 traps in 1 night. Once again, this just shows you the value of the #110 conibear. 70% success in one night is pretty darn good.

Otters

Otters are cool to watch in the wild and are a fun–loving, high-spirited animal. But don't let their fun-loving attitude fool you. They are no slouch in a fight. I have seen them drive a coyote off from a kill. The otter, being a smart water loving animal, will try to lure the coyote into freezing water hoping the ice will collapse under their weight. The otter isn't worried about the cold water and knows the coyote won't last long in it. Otters are smart and fast, and one of the best fish hunters in the wild.

Male and female otters will usually stay together and it is not unusual to see a whole family together. But normally, by the time winter comes along, the young head off on their own. The female normally gives birth to a small litter of 2 - 4 pups. The male will help her with food and the chore of teaching the young.

Some trappers will gang set for them, setting 4 - 6 traps in a single location. And much like the bobcat, they may only come through once a month, depending on weather and ice conditions. So you may only have one shot at them before freeze-up.

My favorite location is a small side stream that leads to beaver ponds. The otter love to hunt these locations one last time before freeze-up. I'm talking about small streams anywhere from one to two feet wide. But I have also caught them on larger  streams and rivers as well. Patience is the name of the game with otter. There is an old saying about otter trapping: "if you see otter tracks, you are too late to get them". That's very true because of the huge hunting circle they routinely make.

People that raise fish down south are good folks to ask for trapping permission, because a family of otter can kill and eat thousands of dollars worth of fish in just a few nights.

Some trappers like the #220 and #280 conibear for otter, but I prefer to use the #330, setting the small streams and springs they like to hunt. Another good location is the slides. Otters will run up the side of banks and slide down into the river. A word of advice here: do not set the slide itself. Since the otter are sliding down at a fast rate of speed, they will normally knock the trap over, setting it off. Now you have a trap shy otter to deal with that will avoid #330 conibears or leg holds. You want to set where they are climbing out of the water to run up the hill. Otters are strong, powerful animals. So using a #3 leg hold on a drowner, set for deep water, is another good tactic.

A friend of mine got started trapping one season, and forgot to take the safety pins off of the #330 conibears he was using. When the otter (one of a pair) hit the trap, it only fired half way, never closing completely. Needless to say, those otters were both trap shy after that experience. He kept an eye on them and observed them as they approached another #330 he had set earlier. They both climbed out of the water and ran along the bank until they had passed the trap safely. When trapping otter with #330 conibears, cover the top of the trap well to break up the outline. That will really make the difference between success and failure. In a pinch, you can also snare otters with a small 6" loop, set 2" off the ground.

If they are legal to trap in your state, they can be a big money critter for you. However, the prices have fallen from the once high $150 per pelt they used to bring in. These days, they are still bringing in around $75. Otters are a good animal to trap for survival reasons, because reducing otter numbers will increase the amount of fish available for you to catch and eat.

Bagging Beaver with the Conibear #330

The #330 conibear is the best beaver trap ever made, and I've taught several people to trap with it over the years. The following year after I taught one of them (and he was only using 6 traps), he caught 18 beaver in the first week. That's really good for a beginner. I have a friend that used to joke that we could trap bear with them. Of course, that's not really possible, because a full sized bear would pull right out.

You can also use the #330 for ground hogs. A recent e-mail I received said to place the #330 over the ground hog hole and the next day the problem is solved. I know of one trapper that used them for culvert trapping in the country. He was trapping wilderness logging roads where dogs weren't a concern. His catch was impressive and included raccoons, otter and beaver.

The #330 is an awesome beaver trap!

The whole idea behind using conibears is to give the animal a reason to stick his head in or try to go through the conibear, like in a culvert. If you want to trap beaver, the best set is the dam crossover. Beaver will dam the creek or river in a spot with slow-moving water. They will have a path along the top of the dam that they use to cross over the dam. This path is easy to spot and sometimes it is so muddied up from the beaver sliding down, it's hard to mistake. The beaver even provide the stabilizing sticks. Make sure you use old sticks because if you grab green sticks with bark on them the beaver might try to grab the stick instead of going through the trap. Just go up to the crossover and place the trap so that the bottom half of it is in the water. Take two sticks and push them through the set springs at a 45-degree angle so they form an "X" over the trap. This prevents the beaver from knocking the trap over. Then take about 6 feet or more of wire and wire it to something solid. Then set your next trap on the bottom side of the dam.

On the bottom side, if there is a fallen old log or branch the beaver are swimming under, make sure you set there. I have had beaver walk around my top set and then swim into the bottom set because it was fully under water. The reason for the long wire is to give the beaver enough room that as he's fighting the trap he pulls out into deep water and sinks. This hides your catch and helps to not spook the other beaver. When I first started taking large numbers of beaver, I didn't do this and after the first beaver was caught on the pond, sometimes the rest of them would refuse to swim near any traps. Or worse, one would come up and slap the trap with his tail until it fired. This would leave you with a sprung trap and no beaver. Wire is cheap, so use it to give the beaver plenty of room to reach deep water and sink out of sight.

The next best set for beaver is where the beaver have dug a channel about 18 inches wide up to a quarter of a mile long. This will have anywhere from 2 feet of water at the beginning, down to just mud at the other end. Find a spot all narrowed down along this path and set the conibear there. After you set the trap, use grass, leaves and small sticks to help camouflage the trap. Remember to blend the trap in with its surroundings. The only problem I've had with this set is predators eating the dead beaver before I check the traps. I have had black bear run off with my traps and found them hundreds of yards away with a half-eaten beaver still in them. Bobcat have pulled the beaver out and eaten and clawed them up. Predators will eat your catch, so if you can, set near the water's edge and give the beaver plenty of wire to reach deep water. If the water is too deep then you can place what's called a 'dive stick' over the trap. Say you have 18 inches of water and the trap is set on the bottom with 6 inches of water over the top. Just take three or four 1 inch diameter sticks and shove them in just above the trap, then place a larger 4 to 6 inch diameter stick on the very top. This will cause the beaver to dive under the sticks right into the trap.

Beaver are wonderful animals to trap, and I trap the Canadian way of taking no more than two beaver from each den. That way, every year you can go back and take two more beaver. This is just a general rule, because I have trapped two beaver and that was it. But, with good trapline management you can keep the beaver there year after year. I call it 'money in the bank', and it's definitely fur on the stretcher!

If you're trapping a wilderness area where dogs aren't a problem, you can build large boxes out of sticks and branches 18 to 36 inches long all narrowed down to just the size of a #330 at the front and bait in the back. There's one thing about conibears that you should always remember: If you're trapping on dry land, you will have to deal with freezing conditions. The trap can freeze to the ground and it won't fire. To prevent this, place small sticks under the trap jaws in order to get the trap off the ground just high enough to prevent it from freezing in place. Some wilderness trappers have this style of sets all over and they catch bobcat, fisher, raccoons and a few foxes and coyotes. Always remember the wind when making this type of set. The trap has to be in the right direction for the wind. If the animal is coming into the sides or back of the box, then you have the door facing the wrong way for the wind. The wind should always come from behind the box, so that the smell of the bait is coming out of the front. The wind is a gamble, so all you can do is make your best guess based on past experience. For example, the wind in November in my area typically comes from the North, so that's how I set up.

Chapter 6: Snaring

Snaring has been around for centuries. You can find references of snaring in the Bible. But with modern advancement, the systems have improved over the years. Some folks who only get their information from TV think of snares as cruel barbaric tools used to trap endangered species in Africa. The centuries old methods being used in Africa are not the same thing as today's modern self-locking snares. The ones in Africa are crude old methods where the foot is snared. I'm not talking about foot snaring, nor do I recommended it. What I want to cover is neck or body snaring.

First, you need understand how a modern snare works. Most people think of some TV show where the animal is snared and then a branch whips him off the ground. Well, that's just not how it works.

For the life of me, I don't understand why people don't buy 10 dozen snares to put away for survival. They are really cheap considering all they can do for you. Here's a Duncan Long Quote for you – "Traps and a good garden will provide more food than a wealth of hunting rifles". Think about it. How much money did you spend on a good deer rifle, scope, sling and ammunition? Over $500 or maybe much more. Many folks think that since they've hunted their whole lives that they can survive. That is not reality, it's a pipe dream. If the end of the world happens, think about it for a minute. Millions of people will be trying to survive. People with limited knowledge will head to the woods and soon every animal will be in constant fear and you will never see them. Within a few months, most, if not all of the backpack survivalists will be dead or gone. That's just common sense. A single deer would only last 1 month feeding two people. What are you going to eat for the rest of winter?

During the Great Depression, many a trapper survived from selling furs and eating the meat. Once the herd of pack survivalist learn they couldn't make it, the well prepared person will be able to add greatly to their food supply with traps and snares.

The modern snare is self locking, meaning the animal is the trigger. Once the snare is worked properly, the animal hitting the snare will close the loop.

Snare Terms:

What is a professional grade self locking snare? Here is a picture of one.

Starting from the top left is the swivel, and inside the swivel is a stop button. To prevent the stop button from getting torn up, a washer is directly under the stop button and functions like a bearing by allowing the swivel to move freely when an animal is caught. On the right hand side, right in the middle, is the support collar. Its job is to hold the snare at the correct height. Next is the sure-lock. This design is based on the Thompson design. Its job is to close securely, and once hitting the animal to lock, so it can not re-open. Last is a stop button, which holds the loop to the sure-lock.

The wire is secured to a branch very tightly so the snare won't twist. You can also skip the support collar and just crimp the wire on the snare. The wires purpose is to keep the snare cable from moving and to support the snare at the correct height. This

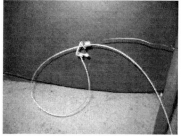

way, when an animal hits the snare, the only thing that moves is the loop as it closes.

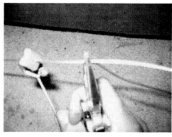

The wire is not a field anchor. A field anchor is very simple. You wrap it around a green tree and put the loop and lock through the swivel, which fastens the snare securely to the tree. The size tree you fasten to depends on what you are snaring. A rabbit can be held by a ¾" sapling. For coon, a 2" sapling is fine. For deer, you should use a 4" sapling, at the very least.

With the small game snare, you can catch 2-3 animals before the cable has to be replaced. On the medium and emergency only deer snare, you most likely will only get one use out of it. That's a small price to pay for all that nice meat.

To repair the snare, you cut off the stop button and save the sure lock, support collar, swivel and washer. Using the proper sized cable from your maintenance kit, take two stop buttons and put the snare back together. I highly recommend you have a new one on hand to use as an example. Pound the stop button on with a hammer and you're back in business. Some folks don't like this fact about snares, but it will save you money and time in the long run. Learn to be as self-sufficient as possible, or you may find yourself doing without.

But let's think about this for a minute. Say you are starving and you just caught a deer. How much is that deer worth to you? $100? $1000? Only you can answer that question. Now consider what an emergency snare kit can catch for you. The total kit weights about 3.5 pounds and can catch two -150 pound deer, six - 15 pound raccoons, three - 2 pound rabbits and three 1 - pound squirrels, just as an example. So that's potentially 399 pounds of meat! Maybe there was one fat squirrel so you can call it 400 pounds. :-) And if you have the repair kit, you can do it more than once. Think about that.

Now just because you have the tools to catch these animals, that doesn't mean you will be successful. If there are no animals left to be caught, then you won't catch any. Another reason is hard to explain because of all the little details. That is why buying the DVD and seeing the actual sets made and the actual catches will have you catching animals faster. Seeing everything in detail will get rid of those little doubts in your mind that come up, causing you to question yourself, wondering if you're doing this right. It will take practice, and you have to be determined to figure it out, but once it clicks you will be so glad you learned the fine art of snaring.

Snared skunk

Setting snares for success

Pick a natural narrowed down spot in the animal trail. In this case a rabbit trail.

Feed the snare around a strong healthy branch. This is for rabbits. For larger animals like coons or coyote you would want a heavy 2-4 inch sapling.

The snare is now secured to a branch. A rabbit doesn't have the strength to tear this loose. Just use common sense here.

Support the snare using 16-gauge wire. Bend a small loop in the snare end and secure it to the snare. The top is wired tight to the branch above. This is very important; make sure the wire does not swivel or spin on the branch.

The support wire is pushed into the support collar. The purpose is two fold, it keeps the snare at the correct height and LOCKS the snare cable so the only thing that moves is the snare loop. The cable behind the lock should not move at all when you test the snare. If it does move, twist the support collar on tighter.

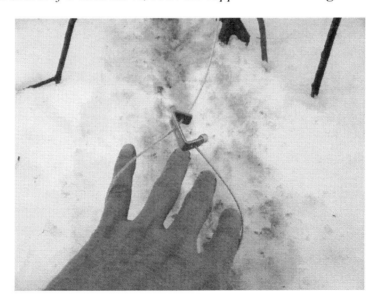

Once set up, test the snare and make sure the only part of the snare that moves is the lock closing on the animal.

Finished and ready to snare the next rabbit that comes through. Make sure the snare loop covers the middle of the trail. This picture should help you take what you have learned about animal loop size and height and adapt to the correct snare, and you are in business. The two most important things in snaring are make sure only the snare closes and no other part of the cable should move. Also, make sure you are covering the center of the trail. Use a guide stick so the only choice for the animal is to go through the snare. Once this clicks in your head, you are all set for learning more and taking a lot of animals.

Always comply with state trapping and snaring laws. Some states require you to use a break-away device so that if livestock is caught in the snare they can break free. The device is normally set to release at 285 pounds of pull, so the snare will still hold the animal you're trying to trap. But a larger animal will break the snare apart and escape. Other states require that your snare have no larger than a 12" loop, and it must be set up so the snare can't open any larger than that at any time. Many states require that you use deer stops so the loop will close to no smaller than 2" – 3". That way, if a deer is caught by the foot, the snare will close down only so far and the deer can easily pull his foot out.

Beavers are easy to snare.

The two most common snare-line problems are 'knock over' snares and 'almost closed' snares with no catch. With new modern support collars, many of the problems can be solved by using a tapered collar design, which can be used with any size wire from 16 gauge all the way up to the large heavy #9 wire. Using this support collar, you can insure that the snare is supported at the correct height and locked on so only the loop will close. Did you work the snare up properly? Does it close fast and smooth? The 'almost closed' snare problem is caused by the wrong animal tripping the snare. Rabbits are famous for hitting the snare with their back feet, causing the snare to close partially, and they're able to escape. Deer will also knock over a lot of snares too.

Double-catches on beaver dams are common, especially when trapping deep in the woods. Snaring coons in areas where hunters frequent can be done by luring the animal off the ground. Find a tree leaning at a 45 to 80 degree angle and place the snare about 4' off the ground. Setting the snare on the tree is a great location because as the coon climbs the tree, it is lined up with the snare and the bait is about a foot higher than the snare. That forces the coon to go through the snare while investigating the bait. Using a small loop, neck catches are common in this type of set.

This picture shows the coon dead as a hammer, hanging clean and dry. The snare wasn't torn up so it can be re-used. This site is located in a wood lot next to a cornfield.Trails leading from old outbuildings are great locations to cover with a snare.

Snaring coyotes

The 6 foot surelock is a great snare and so is the 7 foot camlock. Make sure you check and comply with your state regulations. Many states have mandatory break-away device rules in place so livestock can break the snare and escape. But they still need to be strong enough to hold a coyote.

The same areas that attract fox attract coyotes. Coyotes have a mode of dispersal too, it's just later in the year. Certain pups are allowed to stay in the pack, while others are driven out and sent out on their own. There is an old Indian saying; "when everything in the world is wiped out, the coyotes will still survive'. That's a very wise saying, because the coyote is still with us after all this time. In fact, one study in Texas found you had to kill 73% of the coyote population to affect the numbers. They estimated that if you took 70% of the population, the next year the same number of coyotes would still be there. Why and how? This is a miracle of nature. It happens with fox, coyotes, and wolves. Mother Nature allows for larger litters and more females in the litters. It is truly amazing that nature can adapt this way. But, it's also more proof why trapping is beneficial to the over all eco-system. Newer, younger families are less likely to be prone to disease.

Don't worry about the coyotes, take as many as you can each and every year. There will be plenty more next year. I could write a lot about the coyote and different tactics, but this book is more geared toward survivalist trapping. Just remember, for every coyote you catch, you just saved 10 deer, 100 rabbits, and 20 ducks and 20 pheasants. I think those good eating animals look better in your freezer, don't you?

Snaring Fox

Snaring fox is simple. They will normally fight the snare until they are dead. Use an 8 inch loop, 8 inches off the ground and if you set up right, you should have success.

First, decide which animals you want to snare, and set the snare up for each type. See the table below.

Animal	Snare type	loop size	bottom of loop off the ground	top of loop off the ground
- Raccoon -	3/32 sure lock	8" loop,	2" – 3"	10-12"
- Beaver -	3/32 sure lock	12" loop,	2" -3"	14"
- Squirrel -	1/16 sure lock	3" loop,	½"	3 ½"
- Opossum -	Same as coon			
- Skunk –	1/16 sure lock	6" loop,	2"	8"
-Ground Hog-	1/16 sure lock	7" loop	2"	9"
- Rabbit –	1/16 sure lock	5" loop,	1-2"	7"
- Snowshoe Hare –	1/16 S.L	6- 7" loop,	1"	7-8"
- Coyote –	3/32 cam or surelock	12-15",	10"	22-25"
- Fox –	3/32 surelock	8" loop,	8"	6"
- Deer –	3/32 camlock	16" loop,	15"	31"
- Wild hogs –	3/32 camlock	16" loop,	6"	22"

Chapter 7: Survival Trapping

As a good survivalist, you must learn to recognize natural food sources. Most areas of the country that have water and cattails will have muskrats. In small ponds, lakes and even slow moving streams and rivers, you will find muskrat houses. Around many of cities in America, there are drainage ditches, ponds and streams. These areas are loaded with muskrats, rabbits and squirrels. As an urban or rural survivalist, knowing where to find this food is important. Millions of people drive right by these every single day and never see the food source. To set the sites, take along a couple #110 conibears and a burlap sack, dress in old clothes and jackets, and you'll look like you are collecting cans. The vast majority of the people will never look twice at you.

So, learn to hide in plain sight. You can run your traps, collect your food, stuff them in the bag and walk out. It would be a good idea to have 12 or more cans and hide the muskrats under them in case you are stopped. If the police do notice the muskrat, just tell them you save them for dog food when you find them. Must have been hit by a car, officer (grin). That goes for rabbits, squirrels or raccoons in your bag as well. You are using kill traps, so there's no need to carry a gun.

The houses, or huts, are normally built in October, and I would bet down south maybe as late as November. The houses are built from whatever type water plants are handy, and mud. I believe the muskrat is a distant relative to the beaver. It makes sense, because their huts/lodges are very similar. The hut will come in many different sizes from the small 2' diameter to the large 6' diameter monster you will occasionally find. On average, they tend to look like the picture above.

The entrance is underwater, and is normally found on the deep water side. A small 6" wide trench leads to the entrance of the hut. In really clear water, you will notice the trench will be visible up to 6' or more from the entrance. Understanding the reason the trench goes out so far from the entrance comes through careful study. How does a muskrat enter and leave the hut? And why is that important? Because, the muskrat is the rabbit of the water. Every predator animal is after it; hawks, owls, mink, coon and if caught on land, foxes and coyotes. The predators know what the muskrat hut looks like. So to avoid being caught leaving the hut, the muskrats have learned over past generations to leave and enter the den in a hurry. They shoot out or in along the bottom, getting some distance away before surfacing. This knowledge can be used to your benefit. If you need food in a hurry, and know where there is a large den, you can set one or two #110 conibears in the trench about 2 feet apart. Hopefully the first one caught won't flop into the next one. But it is not uncommon to catch doubles in a set-up like that. Now, you need to remember that muskrats are moving quite fast so you must make sure your stake is firm in the mud, and angled through the top corner of the square part of the conibear. Then securely wire or stake them off.

I have actually witnessed a muskrat getting caught in one of my traps before. He swam up to the trap and slowly backed off about 5 feet, then took off like a shot trying to blast through it! Needless to say, he didn't beat the trap. A little splashing, followed by calm. It was all over in under ten seconds.

During the time of first ice is the very best time to find where the muskrats live. Just follow the air bubbles. You can find the entrance to large huts and even bank dens with this method.

Note the concentration of air bubbles in the picture. Once the ice become thicker, the bubbles may no longer be visible. But if you are on long-term survival, you would want to go around and stake every den like that you could find. Because, then even after the ice becomes thicker, you can go back and located the dens because they're marked.

Before freeze-up, a great location to set your #110 conibear is in the trail leading up to what is known as a feed bed. Feed beds will be found in thick cover; again, remember the muskrat enemies - hawks and owls being #1 on the list - the muskrats learn to stay under cover in the thick cattails. Walk through these areas and you will find them easy enough.

See the fresh green cattail stalks? This tells you there have been recent visits to the feed bed. Note the trail through the cattails. Setting a #110 conibear in the trail, half in and half out of the water, should take the next muskrat that comes through.

Another place to trap is a muskrat toilet. They may feed here or just rest and mark the area. Here is a good example of one. Again, note the fresh green cattail stalks and the brown droppings? The trail leading to this spot is great trap location.

So you see, successful trapping is learning the animals habits, and noticing the details. How many hunters would even think about muskrats for food? Not very many, but the poor muskrat gets a bad rap because of his name: Muskrat. But in reality, hc cats about the same thing a rabbit does; mostly cattail roots and small clams, another food they really like. Muskrats have dark red meat, and are quite tasty to eat. They're high in protein and make a great survival food that is often overlooked by a vast majority of people. The other part that really turns people off is the smell when cleaning them. Skinning them is not so bad, but when you open them up to remove the guts, you will think that's the worst smell in the world and the meat must be bad. Nope, they called them 'musk'-rat for a reason. :-)

Notice the conibear hit the muskrat about mid-body. That means he was coming into the den at a high rate of speed when he hit the trap and died really fast. I also learned that standing on a muddy bottom trying to balance a camera as I hold the muskrat is a lot harder than I thought (grin).

Once you gain experience using this trapping technique, you should be able to reach a 50% catch rate. That means that on the first night you check your traps, if you set four #110 conibears in the den entrances, you should have two muskrats, which is 50% of four traps. Even before ice forms, the entrance is fairly easy to find. Wear hip boots and walk slowly around the den until you feel the drop off of the tunnel. I tested my theory today on the den I was setting, and the trench was roughly 5" deeper than the bottom surrounding the den. Using your foot, follow the trench up into the den and locate the side of the den wall. Set the #110 conibear right in front of that hole. If you are in a really good spot, a 75 to 100% catch rate is possible.

Ok, you have success; now what? Well, now you have protein (neat), fur and bait. Learn to skin the animal and save the fur. I think muskrats have the best fur for many different uses. It's super warm and soft, with a shiny brown color. It's great for hats, mittens, fur lining in coats, and can be sewn inside the legs of loose fitting pants, for great emergency long johns.

Skinning the muskrat.

Because of fur market rules, muskrats have to be case skinned. This means you hang it up by both back feet and make a cut from leg to leg, starting at one paw and ending at the other. As you cut around the leg, be careful not to cut the tendon, then use your fingers and work the pelt down past the legs to the root of the tail. Once you have the hide separated from the hind legs, work your finger through to separate the hide from the meat, then place your knife in the opening and cut upwards to sever the hide from the tail.

Now set the knife down and work your finger down along the backbone, separating the hide as you go. Then switch to the belly side and use the knife to carefully cut along the fat and hide, pulling the skin toward you as you work it apart.

Once you are a little ways down the body, you can grab the hide on each side and work it back and forth, pulling alternately down on one side, then the other. Now don't pull too hard or you will rip the guts open (and trust me, you don't want that to happen). If

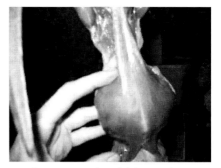

you hit a tough part, carefully cut between the hide and meat with the knife, making sure not to cut the hide. Once you are at the rib cage, you should be able to pull the hide back and forth, all the way down to the front legs. Push your fingers through and pop the feet out on both legs. Now you go back to pulling back and forth until you reach the head on the front side.

At this point, you should see the eye cartilage. With a sharp knife, cut through both ears as close to the skull as you can. Work your way down to the eyes and once again, using a sharp knife, carefully cut around the eyes until the hide separates cleanly from the eye sockets. Once your past the eyes, pull the hide tight towards the nose and use the knife like a saw until you hit the nose cartilage. Then cut straight across until the nose comes off. At this point, the hide should come cleanly off of the animal. You'll use this same method for all animals that require case skinning. The only difference is that on some (like the coyote) you have to pop the tail.

To flesh the muskrat hide, put it on the fleshing beam and push the fat off with a fleshing knife. Then place the hide on stretcher to dry, or put it in a tanning solution.

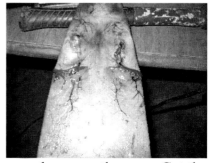

Cleaning the rest of the animal is like gutting a rabbit. Remove the intestines, heart and lungs. Then spilt the hip bones and remove the anus. Cut the feet and head off and wash the carcass and you are ready to cook. That wasn't so difficult, was it? It just takes a little practice. You'll get the hang of it if you stick with trapping. Hey, no one else is going to do it for you. And trust me, it's worth every minute you spend learning how to do it.

Lets say you have 10 ponds in your area within walking distance of each other. One pond has ten muskrat huts, one has eight, one has seven, three have five huts, and two have three huts. And the last two ponds have two huts. Or maybe you have one big marsh with 50 huts total. If you want the animals every year for as long as the water holds out, you only want to take three muskrats per hut or 150 muskrat total, in either situation. A small-time trapper should be able (with only ten #110 conibears) to have this done in 30 checks. Say you average five muskrats per day. It would take you 30 days to finish your trapping. It is easy to put this down on paper, but in reality, things happen that can change your expected average. You might lose permission to trap one pond and someone else may already be trapping another one. Life happens; you have to learn to adapt and just set up more ponds in other areas. Of course, you could have 20 traps set out that are taking ten muskrats a day, and be done in 15 days. Or perhaps 40 traps and be done in seven days. Obviously, it can depend on many different factors. You just have to decide how you want to trap. If it's just a hobby, then treat it like one. But when trapping for survival, you should try to trap a little every year to maintain your skills. Consistently working your trapline will be the best teacher.

Setting the #110 Conibear

Ok the #110 conibear is a like a rat trap a quick kill trap that the rabbit tries to run through with his body and the trap closes around his neck or body killing him quickly. That is why I stress so much for newbie's to order the video. I can not tell you how frustrating it is for folks who say they can figure it out. Below is the sequential step-by-step setting instructions for the #110 conibear. It's the smallest of the conibears and it's really pretty easy to set, requiring no special tools like the larger ones.

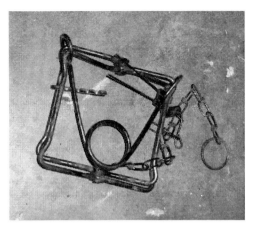

#110 with spring folded.

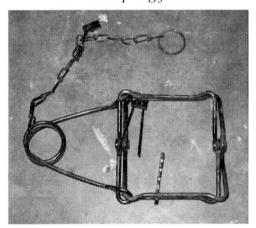

#110 with spring open

Squeeze the spring closed with your right hand and pull open the jaw with your left.

At this point, apply more pressure with you left hand to bring the jaws together.

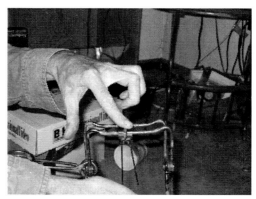

Flip the notch lever up and hook in the notch on the 2 prong trigger.

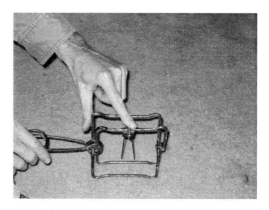

Keep pressure on the notch part to prevent the trap from firing.

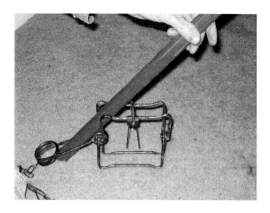

Bend the spring down and place stick as shown. This holds the trap upright in the field.

The stick is to show a rabbit trying to go through the trap head first. The trap fires, killing rabbit.

BE the Bunny: Think like the Animal You Want to Trap.

In this fast-paced world, it's easy to get caught up in the rush of day to day life. People forget to stop, take a deep breath and really think before they act. If you want to step off the merry-go-round into the woods, you must first learn to slow down and t - h - i - n - k. You have to learn to not only *look*, but to *see*. Trapping and snaring success comes through paying attention to the details, not just looking at the big picture. You must learn to think like the animals you are after.

For example: rabbits (the other white meat). Most people who trap think of a rabbit only as survival food; but they're quite tasty and high in protein! They're well worth learning how to trap/snare. So, now that you have a good tasting target, how in the world do you think like a rabbit?

Rabbits have the same basic survival requirements as people: food, water, shelter and mates. Rabbits…breed. I know this will shock you as much as it did me, but it is not uncommon for a single female rabbit to have three litters of 4-6 kits in a year. Just on paper you're now looking at an average of fifteen new rabbits per mating pair per year. Wow!

But this is where thinking like a rabbit begins. What predators are preying on them? Normally, hawks, owls, feral cats, weasels, mink, foxes and coyotes are all capable of taking rabbits. In most situations, even after the predators have taken their toll on rabbit numbers, there should still be roughly 30% - 50% of the new rabbits left to harvest when hunting season rolls around. Predators are not perfect; they make mistakes (like missing their prey) all the time. And each time a prey animal escapes attack, it learns to protect itself better through these near misses. So, if you understand the rabbits basic shelter requirements and defense against predator attack, you can use that information to your advantage.

I listed hawks and owls first because they take lots of rabbits while hunting – "silent death from above". One of my most incredible hunting memories is one where I watched a great horned owl take a rabbit. It was an awesome sight that I will never forget. With a wingspan over three feet, the owl looks huge. Owls tend to sit high in the trees, silently surveying their hunting ground for any movement. They sit motionless for hours at a time, moving only their head. When a rabbit makes the critical mistake of moving slow in the open, the owl swoops down, flaps his wings just before impact and grabs the unsuspecting rabbit in its razor sharp talons. When the rabbit is 'hit', it gives off its death squeal. I believe this accomplishes two things: First, it is an attempt to scare the predator. Second, to warn the other rabbits there is a predator in the area.

When you witness such an event first-hand, you get a clear sense of just how cruel nature can be. I have seen an owl hold down a struggling rabbit, ripping the flesh from its body and eating it while it is still alive. It's a difficult thing to watch. The rabbit dies very slowly, in agonizing pain. The owl may take his prey up into a tree or stay on the ground to finish his meal. Another interesting fact is that owls don't come back to a kill after the first night. As far as I can tell, it's a basic survival trait owls are born with. The fresh blood attracts other predators; and an owl sitting on the ground would make a good meal for a bobcat, coyote or fox.

If you own private property, one thing you can do to increase the small game population is to make brush piles in out-of-the-way places. (Author's note: be careful in dry climates due to forest fires.) When you harvest trees for firewood, make stacks out of the remaining small branches. Make a lot of brush piles across your property, as this gives rabbits more protection. More protection equals more rabbits.

You can also plant 'rabbit favorites' like raspberry bushes, crab apple trees, hawthorn bushes and Russian olives. If you are planting food for your family to eat you want to keep them separate. Wild game plantings should be kept towards the back part of the property, and the fruit trees and berry bushes close to the house for you and your family. The rabbits learn to stay out of the open and hide under something that provides them with overhead protection.

Some like to build 6" x 6" x 24" boxes out of scrap wood instead, or increase the size to 8" x 8" for attracting the larger Snowshoe Hare in Northern climates. Set the boxes out before you use them as traps, as this allows the rabbits time to get used to them before trapping season. Then simply set a #110 conibear or snare on both ends of the box and you're in business.

Other options are to use old culvert or other pipes up to two feet in diameter; just narrow the entrance with brush down to 5" – 6". If you want to make the sites more attractive, you can feed them a little corn now and then. Place the boxes or pipes in the edge of your brush piles. Now, if you were paying attention, I just gave you a big tip for choosing set locations. Culverts, both dry and wet, are used by animals all the time. But, realize you will often have a variety of animals all using the same culvert for shelter. You may set a rabbit snare in front of one and come back to find a torn up snare with no catch. You just ran into a raccoon.

And just because there is a culvert under a road doesn't automatically mean that animals are using it. You still have to have the rest of what an animal needs in area for the culvert to attract game. A culvert in an open area may not have a single animal using it; whereas a culvert near a stream, woods, or crops may be used by several animals. One of the hardest things for people to understand about trapping and snaring is that there are no hard and fast rules. You have to be flexible and learn to adapt to your area just as the animals do.

Trapping predators in your area: fox, raccoons, coyotes, weasel and mink, will increase your rabbit count. But remember that owls and hawks are protected species, and cannot be hunted, trapped or snared!

Once you start to think like a rabbit you will begin to notice rabbit trails through the grass, heading towards the thicker brushy areas. These trails make great set locations, especially under a branch with two narrowed-down sides. I often hear people say: "I can't find a spot like that in the woods". The answer to that situation is simple; make it yourself. Add sticks on both sides of the trail and an overhead branch that sits 7" – 8" off the ground. Set your snare 2" off the ground with a 4" – 5" loop.

Rabbits live most of their lives in a one square mile area. They'll have literally hundreds of trails within that one square mile. How do you know which trail they use every night? Figuring that out takes knowledge, and knowledge comes from practice and experience. You could spend a lifetime just studying the rabbits  in that one square mile, and still not be right every time. That is why I say traps and snares are a percentage game. The more you set out, the better your chances for success will be.

So, what goes wrong with snares? Many things can go wrong. Other animals can come along and knock them over. Or, maybe you didn't work the snare (loosen it up) enough and it didn't close properly, leaving you with a partially closed snare and no rabbit. The rest of the snare could have moved because you didn't secure the support collar correctly and the animal backed out of it. The rabbit may have jumped over the snare because you didn't have a branch or other overhead cover or the overhead cover wasn't thick enough to block his way and force the animal through the snare. What equipment should you use? The 110 is by far the best trap for rabbits, but don't miss the opportunity to practice your snaring skills as well. Every animal you catch will teach you something. Pay attention to the details at each and every set location while running your traps.

Ok, I caught a rabbit…now what? Because they are wild, rabbits have little to no fat on their carcass. Here's my favorite recipe for rabbits:

After skinning and gutting the rabbit, make sure to wash all the fur off of the carcass. Season with your favorite seasonings; I like to use lemon pepper, salt and garlic. Next, add a can of stewed tomatoes, making sure some stays in contact with the meat throughout the baking process. Bake at 350 degrees for two hours, checking every half hour. Baste with tomato juice from the pan each time you check it. Man, I'm getting hungry! You can also cook rabbit like fried chicken with flour and seasonings, cook in a nice stew, or slowly roast on the BBQ grill. Just remember, since the rabbit has no fat, you'll have to add some type of oil or other liquid or it will be dry and tough.

Have fun and "be the bunny!"

What good is survival trapping anyway?

If you are lost in the wilderness and your life depends on you trapping snaring skills to survive, you will be darn glad you learned how.

Now of course because of our lawsuit happy society, here's a big disclaimer: snaring deer, ducks, geese, and in some states rabbits and squirrels is illegal. So the following for informational purposes only.

Got it? You do this stuff and get caught illegally snaring deer or any other animals on the NO list, don't come crying to me. It's your responsibility to check and comply with all state game laws, rules and regulation that apply to trapping and snaring in your area. YOU DO SO AT YOUR OWN RISK. I take no responsibility for YOUR ACTIONS.

Ok now we can get on with this. Any animal can be trapped or snared. Small game snares set up in Duck trails will work like a champ. Camlock snares set in Deer trails are almost guaranteed meat. It is so simple to do that anyone, after watching my Survival snaring Video, can go out and do it if they can recognize a deer trail. That is why it is illegal. Apply what you have learned in trapping other animals to what you want to trap. It is that simple.

The thinking behind the Emergency snare kit.

Many people have asked me why the wide assortment of snares are in my kit, what were you thinking? That is simple. The idea was to make a kit that weighed under 3-1/2 pounds. The kit needs to have enough snares to supply a person with food if lost in the woods, or are involved in a small plane crash, for a month or longer. Kind of a general kit to cover as wide a variety of animals as possible. Squirrels, rabbits, raccoons, opossums, ground hogs, marmots, deer, feral hogs etc... You could even use the small snares for ducks and geese too.

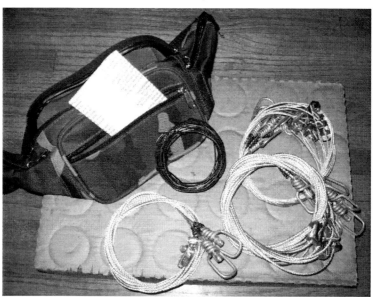

So what can the emergency snare kit do for you? Depending on where you are in the country you could catch 6 rabbits or squirrels, 3 beaver, 3 raccoons, 2 deer or 2 feral hogs if they are in the area. What does this add up to in pounds of meat? Figure one pound each for the rabbit and squirrel, or 6 pounds. Three beaver at 35 pounds each, 105 pounds. Three coons at 15 pounds each, 45 pounds and two deer or feral hogs at 130 pounds each for 260 pounds. So your little 3-1/2 pound snare kits could provide you with 416 pounds of food if there are enough animals in your area. Now add 1 repair kit and you could do it all over again. Now of course, not everyone can just go buy the snares and catch this much food. There is a learning curve while learning to snare. But with my DVD's, most people will manage to catch some animals with this snare kit. Experience is the best teacher. I can only provide you the tools and a knowledge base to get started it is up to you to actually go practice and learn the art. Thinking of trapping and snaring like hunting. If someone buys a gun, that does not automatically make him or her a hunter. Only after actually hunting and gaining experience, does the person learn to become a hunter. Trapping and snaring is the same way. They are awesome wilderness survival tools if you have the knowledge to go with them.

Trust me, when you are starving that raccoon in the snare looks like the best tasting steak in the world.

What else works 24/7 for you and weighs this little bit that can provide this much food? Nothing on the market even comes close. Now think about this; what gun could you carry to do all this that weighs 3-1/2 pounds? Are you going to stay awake 24 hours a day? What happen if you miss?

Once you learn the art of snaring you will have a great understanding of how to quietly, quickly and efficiently harvest wild game for food. With the hard times that are coming down on the Untied States, I highly recommend you learn this skill while there is still time to prepare.

Chapter 8: Survival Fishing And Other Tips

Survival fishing.

I'll bet you never thought you would read about fishing in a trapping book. But, since this is a survivalist/trapping book, I thought I'd put this in her for some interesting (and important) reading. Most folks have heard the joke about the guy who always came home with his limit of fish every single time he when out. He even did better than Bass Pro's tournament guys. Finally, the game warden just had to go out with the guy to find out how he was doing so well. The guy takes him on long boat ride out into the middle of no where and anchors the boat. Then he calmly reaches under the boat seat and pulls out a stick of dynamite and lights it. Then, just as calmly, he hands it over to the Game Warden, who takes it before he knows what he's doing. All the while, the fuse is hissing and sparkling and the Game Warden, all wild-eyed and shaking in his boots, yells; "Fellow, what in the world do you think you're doing!? You can't do that! Don't you know fishing with dynamite is against the law!!!?" The old guy just smiles and says; "Now Warden, are you going to argue, or fish?"

Needless to say, explosives work well for fishing when you're desperate. In fact, I read a book called the 'Thousand mile war'. It was about how Japan had captured Alaska's Aleutian chain all the way to Dutch harbor in WW II. When the Americans finally got around to driving them out, guess who they called on to help? That's right; trappers and woodsmen. They taught the Army troops wilderness survival, and also how to sneak up on and ambush the enemy. I think it was Attu Island where the Japanese soldiers were cut off, and not getting any supplies. The troops were so starving for food that when the Americans bombed the bay and fish floated up to the top, the Japanese soldiers raced out in the water to pick up the fish. Even as more planes were coming in to bomb them. Now that's hungry!

There is a tremendous amount of survival information in the above paragraph. Who did the US Army look to as the true experts in wilderness survival? The trappers and woodsmen. That's a very important statement. Starving people will take desperate measures to get food. They'll even go so far as to face strafing rounds and bombs in order to get something to eat. As a trapper, you must become one with the wilderness. How do I define wilderness? Good question. Wilderness can be defined in several ways; as ten acres just outside of town, or a large farm, or just miles and miles of true wilderness out at the end of nowhere. Learn to study the animals you want to trap, and become the top predator in their food chain. To be successful, you must learn the habits of the animals. And fishing is no different.

Mother earth, or God, or whatever it is you choose to believe, has a truly remarkable plan. Think about it. When spring comes, you want to leave the majority of animals alone. One exception would be spring beaver trapping. So if trapping is limited, what food can you turn to that is usually always available? Fish can fill that niche. Fish have remarkable spawning habits, for the most part. Depending on where you live, certain fish will spawn at different times during the spring. So there can be many different spawning events available for you to take advantage of. Generally, this spawning period will last between 6 weeks to 2 months. In the U.P. of Michigan, the Northern pike are usually the first to spawn. Then smelt, rainbow trout, walleye, bass, and finally bluegills. So during this time of year, the fish can be easy to catch, depending on their habits. Most people know that salmon spawn in the fall, and they run up stream to do it. A lot of different type of fish run up streams and rivers to spawn, but in lakes and ponds, those same fish will come into the shallows to spawn as well. It all depends on the type of fish and the habitat available to them.

Now fish are not smart like some animals, and are fairly easy to trap. Much like when trapping animals, when they are traveling a route you want a natural funnel so they will have to follow to your trap. With fish, funnel them along a bank, and if that happens to be the fishes normal route, you can catch them easily. I talked to an Alaskan trapper once that told me he used a #330 conibear to take salmon. He would remove one of the springs off of each trap and set a dozen along the bank. Then he'd spend all day checking and re-setting traps. He was catching sockeye salmon for his sled dogs. I talked to another guy that put bait right on the trigger of #220 conibears and used them to trap catfish. And another guy who used the #110 conibear baited with smelt, to trap northern pike through the ice.

When suckers were running up stream, I would use #110's and #210's, which only have one spring.

I have studied survival techniques all over the world, and the basic fish trap is the same as a minnow trap you see in bait shops. I have seen them round or even square with a funnel going in. They can be made out of wood, steel mesh, or even slender branches. The wooden ones may have to have a rock inside them for a few days until they are waterlogged and sink, but the concept is the same. Just be sure to match the trap size to the size fish you are after.

Gill nets are awesome fish harvesters to have on hand, but the problem is finding them. Many states have outlawed their use completely. I have gone through 3 suppliers in the past, and can no longer get them legally.

What other methods can you use to catch fish? How about an old hand-cranked, field radio generator attached to two steel rods in the water, about 4 feet apart? I saw the Michigan field biologist doing that back in the 70's, and was shocked to see how many fish floated up to the top. I guess you could use a regular car battery too. Just think about it and use a little common sense before you give it a try. Use rubber gloves and only use a wooden or fiberglass boat or canoe while doing this type of fishing. Think what would happen if one of the rods accidentally hit the side of the boat you and your friends were in? Maybe nothing, but it's possible you could have a light show coming off your hair (grin). And you may not want to use an aluminum handled fish net to dip the fish out , with all that electricity in the water. As always, try this at your own risk. If you become a Darwin Award winner, don't blame me.

What about something a little less work intensive? I've heard that you can remove the green hulls from black walnuts and grind them to a powder, sprinkle it in the water to remove the oxygen, and the fish will float to the surface. Again, a little common sense goes a long way. If you use that method too much on a small lake or pond, you could wipe the fish out completely.

Every state has a few wildlife biologists, and these guys and gals are normally bored and love to show how smart they are in the field. Talk to them. Call them and pick their brains. Ask them when the bass, catfish or other types of fish usually spawn. Listen to these people carefully, because they can give you valuable information. Heck, tell them you are helping your kid write a study paper on fish spawning and improving fish habitat. Tell them whatever you want, but the object here is to learn as much as you can so you can become a better fisherman. When you're hungry, knowledge can make all the difference in the world.

Trotlines have been in use for years. You can pick them up at bass pro shop and many small bait and tackle shops. A trotline is very simple. You have a main line that is very strong, usually 150 pound test. And tied to that are several leaders, each about 2' of braided fishing line in the 20 pound test range. They are normally 100 to 150 feet long with 25 or more hooks spaced evenly. You normally use a boat to set them, one end tied off in shallow water and the other end tied off in deeper water. Use 4 ounce lead fishing weights every 20 feet or so to keep it underwater and out of sight. Bait them with small perch, any type of meat or internal organ chunks and check them every morning and evening.

Another really good toy to have is the yo-yo automatic fishing reel. This is a neat little set-up. You unwind the reel and set the trip lever and when a fish hits and runs it trips the lever and the hook is set. It nice, because it reels the fish in automatically. When the  fish runs, the spring re-sets and it reels him in again and again, until the fish tires out and is there waiting for you. They are great toys to have for camping too because you can stretch them out between two trees and have a ready made clothes line. In a pinch, they can also be used as a snare for small game. Or tie them off to one gallon milk jugs and use them for taking catfish. What could be cooler than an automatic jug line?

For smaller fish a regular plastic pop bottle cap put on fishing line a hook and sinker bait. Toss out in the lake. Now you need a boat for this or you have to tie it off to shore. Fun way to fish cheap and anyone can make them. This should go without saying but most if not all this methods are illegal. So check and comply with all game rules, regulations and laws.

Ten senses

Most folks think everyone has 5 senses; sight, hearing, taste, touch, and smell. The 6th sense is commonly referred to as psychic power. But, in the human world there are actually 10 senses. The remaining five are; feeling, thought, consciousness, memory and experience. But, in the animal world, they use most, if not all of the same senses to stay alive. Let's say a rabbit wanders too close to a fox den. The fox chases the rabbit, but he barely escapes. Let us look at the senses the rabbit will use to escape the fox; sight, running from the fox, hearing the sounds the fox makes as the fox gains ground on the rabbit, and the smell of the fox. Now, what senses will the rabbit use next time to avoid the fox? The rabbit, from learned experience, will use his memory. The fox is a danger he recognizes by sight and smell, and will remember what it heard/smelled.

Some hunters will say big bucks are really smart. This is not true, they are educated because of bad experiences with previous hunters. The average 8 point in Michigan has been shot at 8 times in his lifetime. He will use past experiences, memory that the hunter is a danger he recognizes. The sight, smell, and what he heard. This is in no way giving the deer human knowledge or creative skills. A deer still cannot read. They are animals whose life is full of danger and they adapt and learn to survive in their environment. This is the deer's survival skill in action, and it really comes down to the most basic level of an animals survival skills.

Whether you are trapping, snaring or hunting, understanding the basics of how animals survival skills work will make you a better hunter, trapper, or snaresman. More time and space has been wasted and myths spread about animals ability to smell than can be accounted for. Any bow hunter that has spent enough time in the woods can tell you about deer scenting them and running off. This is a quite common occurrence. Remember, the deer lives in the woods 365 days a year and they notice little details. Little changes they sense alerts them that something is up. They will then scent the air trying to smell you. Their ears will be listening for anything out of the ordinary. The eyes focus on trying to see you. Now this is where experience comes into play. Their memory will be triggered, and the deer's survival skills will kick in.

Most hunters spend a lot of money trying to cover up their scent, but a lot of times, the real problem is something the deer heard. Deer have great big ears and can hear very well. That reminds me of time I was muzzleloader hunting in Michigan. About an hour before dark, I was sitting on the edge of cedar swamp. There was lots of snow on the ground and I was sitting on 5-gallon bucket tucked up against a small pine tree. It was good cover to break up my outline. A doe came out about 60 yards away and I pulled the hammer back with the trigger held back to prevent the gun from clicking. Once the hammer was all the way back, I released the trigger so the gun would stay cocked and be ready to fire. As I slowly released the hammer, I heard a faint click. It shouldn't be able to hear that at this range, about 60 yards. The deer froze with one foot still hung in the air and her head swiveled right around staring at me. I froze. The deer must have been shot at before because the next thing I saw was her turning around running off disappearing into the thick swamp. The wind was in my face. The only thing I could think of that I did wrong was the faint click of the gun. I believe many times hunters make a noise that alerts the deer and that causes failure in the hunt. The bigger bucks have been shot at a lot and learn to avoid these noisy areas. It's not the scent of the hunter.

It's the same with trapping and snaring. People go overboard on the scent issue. Not smoking around snares, only wearing rubber gloves, wearing hip boots and spraying fox urine on their boots. If that is your way of doing it and you believe in it, keep doing it that way. When it comes to traps and snares, the number-1 problem is clean boots. Avoid gas stations, and if you do go to the gas station with your boots on, wash them off in water, mud puddles, wet grass, streams, ponds, lakes or what ever. Handling snares and traps bare handed is really no big deal, especially if you have not picked up a foreign odor like gas, oil, anti-freeze etc. Just keep your hands and boots clean and you shouldn't have a problem.

Human scent is defined in two categories; hot fresh scent and old lingering cold scent. This is easy to explain. Those folks who don't believe in shooting deer try different methods to keep the deer out of their yards by using human hair and urine. The deer know that that hair represents old lingering scent. I would bet it doesn't smell any stronger than lingering scent from you watering and handling your garden plants just before dark. The deer will still come and feed on them. That is why the human hair trick doesn't work, because it is not fresh hot human scent. The lingering human scent on bare metal is said to last 3 hours. This is based on fall temperatures and cooler weather.

But let us think about this for a minute. If the smell of metal and human is something to avoid for animals then why would a raccoon crawl under a chain link steel fence and knock over a steel trash can in order to get a meal? There is fresh human scent on the steel trash can, right? You see we come back to the raccoon or any animal that has experienced metal as no harm and holds good things to eat. He has not had a bad experience or memory of danger from cold lingering human scent. But, if the raccoon had run into a Mickey Mouse homemade snare once in his life that held him for 5-10 minutes, that bad memory would come back any time it encountered a new snare. You see, the animal is not really smart, just educated. Handling that snare with scent free gloves would not make any difference, because the raccoon would use his sight and bad memory to avoid the new snare.

The same applies to any form of trapping, hunting or snaring. Don't do what everyone else is doing. Change makes things look different. Remember the 10 senses and the animal survival skills. Adapt and learn and you will increase your survival skills and trapping success.

Predators: What you should know.

While I was researching for my film 'Unduc Burden, the real cost of living with wolves', I read the 1982 Plan to reintroduce the Mexican Gray wolf. The interesting part was one sentence: In the Country of Mexico, where people are struggling to survive, they do not have the luxury of protecting wolves. As the country slides off into the Great Depression II, people are going to once again hunt to survive and will no longer have the luxury of worrying about predators over human survival. Each wolf kills on the average 35-50 deer a year, along with an untold number of fawns. Why do I say untold? Because the wolves eat everything; hooves, teeth and everything else on fawns. Experts agree there is no way to Judge how many fawns are killed each spring. But it is easy to comprehend when you see doe's with no fawns in the spring. It doesn't take a rocket scientist to figure out predators most likely ate the fawns. Of course there is last years fawns that didn't breed. But if you see ten doe's and only one has fawns, you most likely have a predator problem.

As someone with over 40 years of experience in the woods, I understand how nature works quite well. In the canine world, the fox can be the top canine until the coyotes move in. The coyotes will then run off or kill most of the red fox. Then the coyote is the top canine until the wolf moves in. And the wolves will then kill or run off most of the coyotes. You see this is a pecking order for the food chain. Now man, using real science, has discovered the balance of nature where X amount of predators are harvested every year. This keeps the predator in balance with the land. But the professional environmental groups sue, and stop wolf hunting. The end result is going to be a back lash. I predict the backlash might get real nasty. The rural Americans struggling to survive just to pay their bills and keep food on the table are going to need those 35-50 deer eaten by each wolf each year.

But wherever you live, if you want to increase your game animals you need to thin down the predators. Every coyote you kill is that many more deer rabbits ducks pheasants quail in your area. Same with fox you must become the top predator in your area.

Another big one is hawks, especially the red tail hawk, whose numbers in the U.S. are in the millions. Hawks and owls today are Federally protected birds, so do no harm to them. My cousin was visiting a spot near Lake Superior and they were counting Red tail hawks as they flew south for the winter. In one hour alone, they counted over 20,000. Even the people counting said they are not sure what the numbers are for total population. I am not talking about wiping them out but they need to be thinned down to roughly 2 hawks per 6 square miles. I can hear people screaming now; OMG, he is talking about killing hawks. For the last 30 years, people have been bombarded with nonsense, and brainwashed about nature. Only one side is shown, and the general public overall is clueless about how nature works. Man is part of nature, and as people struggle to feed their families, more people will turn to the land for food. It is only common sense they will kill off the predators to increase their own food supply.

You start trapping and snaring the predators and you will increase your food supply. Don't worry, you can't wipe them out. The coyote has been hunted, poisoned, trapped and snared and they are still here in great numbers. They can take the pressure and bounce back every time. In fact, you will see a healthy predator population has less disease like rabies and that will contribute to an overall healthy wildlife population.

But it's up to you, and if you want to supplement your food supply with wild game you'd better learn how to trap and snare predators. You know I have talked to hunters in areas where I trap, and I just have to smile at their ignorance. They talk about nature, and predators balancing nature, and I tell them "you are seeing the small game population you are because I trap here". They say "that can't be so because predators balance nature". "LOL yes, but who balances the predators? You just told me the hunting has really gotten better in the last 4 years here right"? "Yes why"? "Because that is when I started trapping this area". "Oh". That's when the light bulb clicked on.

Do you have the luxury to allow predators to eat the game that could feed your family? Only you can answer that question, but don't ever ask me "why wasn't I warned about this?" It comes down to whether you're 'Pro-Human' or 'Pro-Predators', because nature doesn't care if you are ignorant about the food chain. If you want to increase YOUR food supply, you'd better start trapping the predators. The real Americans living on the ground will learn to solve the problem. Look at it this way; for every coyote you kill, that means 100 more rabbits available in your area. And it's the same with fox – for every fox you kill, that lets 100 pheasants and 100 grouse survive. For every wolf gone, that is 35-50 deer more a year. Then there are hawks. For every hawk gone, there are more pheasants and grouse available for humans to eat. I read a study years ago about thinning hawks to protect pheasants. In the control area, the hawks were removed by live trapping and in the other area the hawks were left alone. In the controlled area, the pheasants increased 100 % that year and in the other area 20% increase. It comes down to simple math. Studies done proving that predator control is the most effective way of increasing game populations have been buried, and the public is never able (or allowed) to read them or see them on TV.

When your survival depends on it, all the pipedream nonsense about predators will quickly be forgotten. Become the top predator in your area for your families' survival. I was talking to a trapper and he told me about the great small game hunting in his area. His words were;" the local hunters never knew I was trapping the area". That is quite common, because a good trapper keeps his mouth shut and works an area keeping the predators numbers down. It's just plain common sense and once you see it with your own eyes, you will be a true believer that predator control equal more prey species for eating.

Don't Catch Dogs

If you have any doubt in your mind, never set a #220 or #330 on the ground if you think you may catch a dog. I look back over all my years of trapping and the number one problem is people and their dogs. I'm legally trapping and the owner is irresponsible and allows his or her dog to roam free and the dogs get caught in the traps. Whose fault is it? I have caught dogs 8 miles away from the nearest house. This is a sore subject with me, because people tend to stretch the true story. Like one guy I met that was yelling at me when he found out I was a trapper. Here is his story: "You damn trappers; my dog was caught in a trap for 9 days before I found him. Well, I fixed that trapper real good. I busted his trap all up". Here in Michigan, it's illegal to allow your dog to roam free. Nobody checks their traps once every nine days, the law states every 24 hours. But, because of all the negative press on trappers, people just love to say that trapping is cruel, mean and heartless. Later I heard from someone else that the loud mouth I ran into was walking his dog when it got caught. The dog was released un-harmed from the leg-hold, but of course, the story got bigger with each telling until the guy actually believes that is what happened to his poor dog.

FAQ's
(Frequently asked questions)

Q1 - How efficient are the spring loaded reels? The ones that you pull out and set and when they get a strike they release and hopefully get you a fish. How well do they work? And are they cost effective?

A - You are referring to yo/yo fishing reels. Awesome little toy to have around. They're made out of stainless or galvanized steel and last a long time. They were originally developed for down south on the lakes and ponds that are full of panfish. The idea was to attach them to a dock and quickly catch a mess fish for supper. I am really impressed and have had good luck with them. Many of my customers have used them attached to 1-gallon milk jugs for catfishing with awesome results. Very cost effective considering how many years of use you can get out of them.

Q2 – With homemade trotlines, what type of materials are best, how much should the hook hang down, and how should it be anchored or stabilized.

A - 100-150 pound braided line is used as your main line and every 8 feet you tie a swivel on. Off this swivel you attach 3 feet of line mono-filament light line in the 12-20 pound test range. The hook and sinker is attached to this. On a 100 foot trotline you will 12 hooks or you can drop down to every 5 feet intervals with a 2 foot piece of line and have 20 hooks per hundred feet. This is normal stretched out across a lake from the shallow to deep water, sinking the deep end. The idea behind the heavy test is if one is hung up you can break and lose one hook instead of the whole set up. The shallow end is normally attached to a solid branch 2-3 inch diameter sunk in the mud and on the deep end a heavy rock can be attached to sink and hold it in place. Or you can tie it off to 1-gallon milk jug and enough line to allow it to sink to the bottom and then anchor the one gallon jug. Depending on the fish you are after, you can place this several different ways. By suspending it just off the bottom or either just beneath the surface using 3-4 milk jugs along the line to keep the bait up.

Q3 - How good are the small gill nets, how large should they be and how do you use them properly.

A - Gill nets are awesome little toys to have. But don't think you are going to bring home boat loads of fish off a little 4x12 net. You can catch 2-3 fish in them at a time, and in a really good area you might catch 8-10 in a night. Set them the same as you would a gill net. I have set them straight out from shore out toward deep water and caught some real nice bass. I have also put them out near the deep hole coming up to the shallow end and did fairly well. You can also sink them with heavy rocks with floats attached to the top part and sink the net out of sight. On rivers and streams, you put them out in deep holes where the current is slow. Tie one end off to shore and either put a stick in deep water to tie it to or use a rock to sink with a float or two to keep the net spread out. Just remember, never put the net out stretched tight or it won't work. The net has to have give so the large fish can get caught with their large size fins. About 1/3 of the net should be loose.

Q4 - Improvised snares do's and don'ts.

A - Improvised snares are a waste of time and energy unless that's all you have to work with. They work good for ground squirrels and red squirrels. I have tested 22 gauge galvanized wire on cottontails and snowshoe hares and they have broken it. For squirrels, they work as long as you remember to have it on a leaning pole and when the squirrel falls off the pole his back feet must not touch the ground or he can break the snare. Using real modern self-locking snares compared to homemade snares is like hunting with a BB gun as compared to a shotgun. Sure you will get some animals with a BB gun, but with a shotgun you can take animals from as small as a rabbit to as large as a deer. The same holds true with real snares as compared to homemade. You can take anything from rabbits to deer with commercial snares. While with homemade snares you can take squirrels and maybe rabbits if you do the old spring pole method to get pressure on the rabbit.

Q5 - How do you effectively place a snare, and what do you look for to show where you might catch a critter?

A - The main thing with snares is that you set them on a trail, and understand the habits of the animals that use those trails. Always the best snare set up is where the trail naturally goes under a fence, a branch, or even tall grass so the animal is used to ducking or going into a confined area. That's where you want to put the snare. This is covered in more detail in the snaring chapter.

Q6 – How effective are small pocket knives, i.e.: Swiss army non-locking blade type knives?

A - Before the Leatherman and the many other off brands came out, there was the Swiss Army. I carried one myself for years. The originals, made in Switzerland, have awesome steel. I skinned many an animal with mine including fish. Nowadays, the Leatherman, the new SOG, or even Gerber are all good choices. They're very handy on the trapline for cutting wire, cleaning the animals, emergency repairs on vehicles etc...

Q7 - What bait is best for common critters, like squirrels and raccoons? Do I really need to use scents/lures?

A - Raccoons are very curious animals and are always hungry. But like us, they prefer a variety of foods. The idea behind most scents is to have so many wonderful smells that the majority of coons will have to check it out. You can catch coons on any kind of bait but fish works the best. Squirrels are best baited with peanut butter. But pecans, acorns, walnuts and corn on the cob will all work. Cut the corn on the cob to about 2 inch lengths and place on the #110 trigger. That setup will take all kinds of game birds, squirrels and rabbits but never put bait on a #220 trigger for raccoons or they will set the trap off and not get caught. With coons, always have the bait behind the trap so the coon tries to walk through to get at it. I talked to an Alaskan trapper that just put chunks of hot dog on the trigger and caught all kinds of red fox in a #220 this way. If you see the key board commando's saying this will never work just smile. :-)

Q8 – How do I keep from getting rabies while skinning coons and other wild game?

A - Contact the CDC and your local game biologist for the most detailed answer. If rabies is in the area, only skin raccoons in December, January and February. That is the safest time of year to minimize exposure. Wear good gloves when skinning wild game. If an animal appears unhealthy, with blurred eyes, ragged dirty hide and are skinny with a runny nose, or of course are foaming at the mouth, only touch it while wearing gloves and destroy the gloves after you are done. If the world is still together at the time, turn it into your state health department for testing. Rabies can kill you if you are bitten by an animal that is infected. You need to kill the animal and turn it in for testing and get your shots right away to be safe. If the end of the world happens you want to burn the animal in a large, hot fire. This stops the spread of the rabies to other animals by keeping them from eating the dead one. Rabies is spread from saliva, blood or intestinal fluids. A small nick in your hand will allow rabies to enter your bloodstream quickly. Most often, the disease is transferred from being bitten. Bats, skunks, coons, fox and bobcat are the most common carriers.

Q9 - I have the choice between brown or black speed dip for conibears. Any suggestions?

A - Brown is best for real clay type soil where the water has that brown look. Where you are the black will work better.

Q10 – Will mixing Speed Dip with pure clear kerosene work for my fox and coyote traps?

A – No. When it comes to fox and coyotes, they are a little smarter then most other animals. You want to use regular logwood trap dye with trap wax.

Q11 - What does loading a snare mean?

A - Loading a snare is a term use to describe working a snare in such a way that it almost springs closed by itself when an animal hits it.

Q12 - How do you work a snare?

A - When you first get a snare, there are tiny burrs on the lock and cable. You want to open the snare to the correct size you need, holding the snare cable in one hand and the lock in the other, you pull the snare closed. You do that with the lock at a slight angle so it scraps off the burrs but not so hard that you kink the cable. Do this a few times. Then open the loop and form it to a round circle. Practice and play with them a few nights and you will be able to get the knack.

Q13 - What problem do you run into most often?

A - Dogs. People that move to the country and just let their dogs run wild. When I am fox and coyote trapping on farms where I have permission, a lot of farmers will tie their dogs up for me for 7-10 days while I work the farm. It is the neighbor that lets their dogs run free that are the problem. Also, hunters sneaking onto the property without permission causes problems. A catch pole is needed for safely releasing dogs. Using offset jaw traps also helps. People normally calm down after you show them offset jaws and release the dog unharmed. I once caught a little Jack Russell terrier in an Mb650 set for coyotes. He put up quite the yelling fit but finally calmed down and I was able to release him. Within an hour he was walking fine, and within 2 hours he was running around normal.

Q14 - What is Muskrat push up?

A - In Northern climates where the lakes and ponds freeze over, muskrats will make a feed station out a ways from the den. They will push through the ice and actually make like a mini hut where they can come out to get some air and feed. A really good location for trapping is to clear out a hole and set a trap with plenty of wire for them to dive deep when caught. 3 feet of wire tied off to a stick on the outside will do it. Make sure you re-cover it with brush and snow.

Q15 - How do you remember where your traps and snares are set?

A - You break down the woods into sections. Lets say I have 2 traps set next to a large brush pile. On streams you can find different land marks. The best way is to go back the way you came in about 100 yards, and then go find it again right away. Remember the little details; anything that is different. Some folks use flagging to help find snares. That's where you use a small piece of blue tape tied up at eye level. But of course, marked like that, you have to be careful about thieves.

Q16 - Is there a problem with trap theft?

A - Not like there used to be. When fur prices were high, there were always thieves. Most of them are poachers and spotlight hunters as well. While searching the fields for deer, they will come across animals in traps. Avoiding them is always a challenge. During deer season, when the big herds of people are in the woods, I pull my traps for the first few days because of all the thieves. Yes, I have had many a deer hunter shoot and steal fox and coyotes, traps in all. Using drags helps, but with conibears the thicker brush piles are used as natural cover to your benefit.

Q17 - What is the right number of traps and snares to have to supply meat for a family of 6 for 2 years in a "normal" country environment?

A - That's a very hard question to answer without more information. Where do you live? What's the human and animal population? How much other food do you have stored? What are the ages of the people? Maybe 4 teenage boys? If a family that large is in the right area, you will be covering 6-10 miles. You would need a basic food storage system already in place. A big pot of rice with 1 muskrat could feed the family. But if no rice or potatoes or beans you would need 1 muskrat each. See you would have to eat more like the Chinese and carve the meat thin and cook it with rice to stretch it out. For a family that size figure 3-dozen #110 conibears and 15-dozen assorted snares. That should keep them in food for 2 years. If they are in a good area.

Now lets break things down for 1 full year of food. There are 52 weeks in a year, so 1 duck or pheasant a week. That is 52 to catch each year using #110 conibears or shooting them as you check your traps. Each person will need 1 pound of meat like deer, 3 times a week. On the average a deer well give you 80 pounds of meat, leaving all the soup and rib bones for cooking up stock. So that's 156 pounds, and 2 deer will cover that. Then you go for muskrat or rabbit 1 once a week. 52 easily covered with the #110 and snares. We have 5 days covered for the week, so the last 2 days can be covered with fish, turtles, frog legs, squirrel, raccoon, beaver, ground hog etc… But if you were just eating meat you would have to have 5 times as much. That's why it is so important to have plenty of basic food storage; rice, beans, barley, wheat, potatoes.

Q18 Do you have suggestions for urban survival trapping?

A – In an Urban survival situation, dress for the part. One trick I use to do along the highways was dress like a bum. I'd wear big wide pants 3 sizes too big to hide my hip boots. Add and old ratty looking coat, smear dirt on your face if you have to. Pick up a hubcap and everyone thinks you are just collecting cans. Carry a burlap sack with 12 cans in it. Learn to hide your trap locations better using natural blocks and barriers. You have hip boots, so cross the stream or ditch and get off the beaten path. Most folks stay on the path around urban areas and are scared to death about getting off the path. Learn the area. There will be natural dips that someone walking the path would never see your set or catch. Don't make a habit of checking your traps the same time every day. Come into the area from different ways and different times. Even if the cops stop you with traps and snares play dumb like you don't know what they are but figure the scrap guy would pay good money for them.

Q19 - Do you have recipes that you can share? You can mail them to people directly when they email you and you will have their email addresses for marketing.

A - You can make anything taste good by making soups or stews boiled for 1 hour or so. Cool off and strip the fat, break down and mix with what ever you are having that night. Navy bean soup with raccoon is awesome that way. Muskrat on the grill is awesome too. The biggest mistakes people make are from misinformation that the animals carry diseases and they over cook the heck out it. If you are going to do this, slow boil and make stews, and soups. Another big tip is roasting over hot coals, makes for a great meal.

Q20 - Why would anyone eat a muskrat?

A - Muskrats have been given a bad rap. In Louisiana they are known as marsh rabbit. They eat much the same thing a rabbit eats just the underwater roots and greens. But because of the rat tail people can't handle the idea of eating them. But look at the tail, it is flat on both sides and used for swimming. A brown rat seen in the city has a round tail and eats garbage. Skinning them you will find out why they are called Musk-rats. Because of the musky smell when gutting one. Other than that, like squirrel or rabbit, they are a very good source of protein and mostly over looked by other people. In hard times, folks will forget their food prejudges and be glad to have something to eat.

Q21 - Can you really survive off traps and snares?

A - Yes and no. If you are in the right area and have good food stocks stored, sure you can. You can also tan the hides and make hats, gloves, blankets, etc for sale or trade. The big thing is to keep your mouth shut. Never brag about how easy it is or other people will quickly follow you in. When trading it's best to say you have been collecting hides for years and finally have the time to sew them into garments. The 'no you can't survive' part is if you are overrun with people. If 400,000 people hunted every square inch of land they would hunt themselves out of food. Again I have mentioned this many times. It's best to allow the back pack survivalist time to die off or return to the city and nature will come back to normal. Traps, snares, a good garden and stored food will get you through for years if you have enough stored and the ability to grow more. This is meat supplemental for adding to your diet.

Q22 - A friend tried snaring for 2 weeks and never caught a single animal. Why do you suppose that is?

A - When I hear complaints like this I think this person does not have good woods sense. He could have done a lot of things wrong. What happens is I recommend people to buy the snare kit with the DVD so you can see how it works but they get the snare kit and say I can figure out. Then when they fail to figure it out they quit and complain about it. You have to understand the correct way to set a snare, and you have to have the correct animals coming through your area. But if you are one of those guys "I can figure it out", don't go complaining because you didn't figure it out. I have sold snare kits to special forces that have used them very successfully. Get the DVD and go out and practice. Seeing the set made then, followed by the catches it well click in your head how to properly make the set to be successful.

Q23 - How do I clean/gut in the field for meat only?

A - Depends on what you are doing. You don't have to gut unless you want to add fresh bait to a trap site. Because with traps and snares you don't have internal disruptions that causes containmanition. With guts intact you can take the animal home whole.

Q24 - How do I preserve game meat?

A - Preserving meat is a chapter all to itself. Depends on where you live and your outside temperature. Do you have a working freezer? Do you have canning jars, or you can build a smoker to preserve the meat?

Q25 - What is the biggest mistake beginners make?

A - Not buying good equipment. Now good equipment does not necessarily mean the most expensive like Victor traps. They cost the most but the cheap Duke traps work well and in fact have strong steel and springs. The junk Victor did not in the early 80's. Yes I am bitter about the Victors because I spent the extra money for them back then and it cost me thousands of dollars in lost fur because of pull-outs. Today the Bridger, Sleepy creek and MB are outstanding traps. Used traps like the Long spring victors, Blake and Lamb and Newhouse are some of the best. I don't like the coil spring victors and I will never buy another one. I don't care that the company is in new hands today.

Q26 – What's the second biggest mistake?

A - Getting discouraged and not checking the traps every day. Then an animal can be sitting in the traps for days. It is your responsibility to check your traps every day, so if you can't then don't set them. Of course there is exception drowner legholds and conibears can be checked every few days because the animal is dead.

Q27 - Third biggest mistake?

A - Not paying attention to the wind. If more people would worry more about good scent, bait and wind direction, they would be far better trappers. If they cared as much about wind direction as they do human scent it would make a big difference. A lot of disinformation is still floating around today about covering human scent. Worry more about wind direction, lure and bait.

Q28 - Fourth biggest mistake?

A - Not getting permission to trap and sneaking in on private property.

Q29 - Fifth biggest mistake?

A – Not keeping their mouth shut. Other trappers will talk to you but what they are really doing is finding out information about you. Like WHERE you are trapping so they can cut you off. What type of lure you are using, what type of bait you are using, any free tips you might want to give them. I have seen guys that are too nice spend all the money on the books, DVD's and even paid for training give the stuff away. These so called friends are just using you and your money so they can become better trappers. Plus you are learning tricks and tips that took 30 years for me to learn that will increase your catch. If you just give the info out the other guy is catching the animals before you even get a chance at them. Think about it.

Q30 - Sixth biggest mistake?

<u>A</u> - Being cheap on lure. A bottle of lure cost $4 and is designed to be used up in 35-40 sets. It lasts about 7-10 days or after every rain it should be refreshed. Tiny bait misinformation is big time out there. Mice steal and eat a lot of bait. If you are using a small lima bean piece of bait and the mice steal it you are out of luck. Use big pieces of bait. On my mink sets, I will use at least a 4 oz chunk of fish, or 1/4 of muskrat all the way up to a whole muskrat carcass. Same with fox and coyotes. You read that nonsense about using tiny pieces of bait because the smell of large bait will scare off fox and coyotes. Now you know that is disinformation. If that was true, fox and coyotes would not eat from road kill deer. Think about it, it's just plain old common sense. If the target animal doesn't smell your lure or bait, you can't catch them. I remember one story about a guy who didn't lure a set for 40 days and finally caught a coyote in the set, and his conclusion was the lure was still working. Poppycock! The coyote just worked the dirt hole because of the hole. Now if he had been re-luring and re-baiting each week, he might have caught 4 coyotes out of the set instead of just one. Come on folks, use some common sense.

About the Author

Bruce 'Buckshot' Hemming has 34 years of trapping experience and has spent over 40 years in the wilds of America chasing his dreams. His lifelong goal is to share his insight with as many people as he can. He is a wilderness survival instructor with hundreds of students trained personally by him, and tens of thousands trained through his DVD's and books. He currently resides on a small hobby farm in North Dakota.

Buy these titles from his website at: www.snare-trap-survive.com

Wilderness Survival DVD	Trapping DVD'S
Vol 1 - Real Equipment	Survival Snaring
Vol 2 - A Time and a Season	Advance Snaring
Vol 3 - Smoking and other tips	Ultimate Trapping Tips
Vol 4 - Summer Survival	Water Trapping
Vol 5 - Fall Survival	Predator Trapping
Vol 6 - Bug out survival	Advanced Predator Trapping
Vol 7 - Winter Survival	Cleaning Game for the Table